The Business of Writing and Speaking

A Managerial Communication Manual

The Business of Writing and Speaking

A Managerial Communication Manual

Larry M. Robbins, Ph.D.

Director, Wharton Communication Program
University of Pennsylvania

McGraw-Hill Book Company

New York St. Louis San Francisco Auckland Bogotá Hamburg
Johannesburg London Madrid Mexico Montreal New Delhi
Panama Paris São Paulo Singapore Sydney Tokyo Toronto

THE BUSINESS OF WRITING AND SPEAKING:
A Managerial Communication Manual

1 2 3 4 5 6 7 8 9 0 D O C D O C 8 9 8 7 6 5 4

ISBN 0-07-053089-0

See Acknowledgments on page 216.
Copyrights included on this page by reference.

This book was set in Times Roman by Automated Composition Service, Inc.
The editors were Stephanie K. Happer and James R. Belser;
the designer was Joseph Gillians;
the production supervisor was Diane Renda.
The drawings were done by J & R Services, Inc.
R. R. Donnelley & Sons Company was printer and binder.

Library of Congress Cataloging in Publication Data

Robbins, Larry M.

The business of writing and speaking.

Bibliography: p.
Includes index.
1. English language—Business English. 2. English
language—Rhetoric. 3. Communication in management.
I. Title.
PE1479.B87R6   1985   808'.066658   84-15420
ISBN 0-07-053089-0

Contents

PREFACE   vii

PART 1   GENERAL PRINCIPLES OF COMPOSITION

Chapter 1	The Nature and Uses of Communication	3
Chapter 2	Purpose, Audience, and Preparation	14
Chapter 3	Logic, Organization, and Persuasion	34
Chapter 4	The Process of Revision	44

PART 2   SPECIFIC TASKS OF WRITING

Chapter 5	Letters	59
Chapter 6	Memos	74
Chapter 7	Reports	86
Chapter 8	Proposals	97
Chapter 9	Case Analyses	106
Chapter 10	Résumés	117

PART 3 GENERAL PRINCIPLES OF SPEAKING

Chapter 11 Organization   131
Chapter 12 Preparation and Rehearsal   139
Chapter 13 Techniques of Delivery   143
Chapter 14 Using Visual Aids   154

PART 4 SPECIFIC TASKS OF SPEAKING

Chapter 15 Group Presentations   165
Chapter 16 Questions and Answers   171
Chapter 17 Meetings   176
Chapter 18 Interviewing   181

APPENDIX 1 GLOSSARY OF STYLE AND USAGE 189

APPENDIX 2 WORKSHOPS ON WRITING AND SPEAKING 206

BIBLIOGRAPHY 213

ACKNOWLEDGMENTS 216

INDEX 217

Preface

Students and professionals today realize that clear communication is a prerequisite for success, and they need a book that will apply the basic skills of writing and speaking to the problems of business communication. *The Business of Writing and Speaking* is a concise but complete book that integrates basic skills, intellectual inquiry, and specific topics of communication applicable to the professional world.

Before we begin to communicate, we need to know why we are writing or speaking, what we need to say, and what our audience needs to hear. To address these important questions, the first section of this book deals with the general principles of communication, principles that underlie writing and speaking alike. Important features of this section include computer-assisted literature searching and methods of developing logical arguments. With proper research of topic and audience, we can begin to remove the barriers to clear expression.

The second section presents the basic types of written communication: letters, memos, reports, proposals (including fund-raising proposals), case analyses, and résumés. Each chapter includes examples, with suggestions for revising organization and unclear expression.

The section on general principles of speaking offers sensible suggestions for overcoming the problems of stage fright, organization, delivery, and the use of visual aids. Building on the principles introduced in the sections on writing, the chapters on speaking show how an understanding of topic, audience, and personal skills can help speakers become credible communicators.

The fourth section covers the common types of oral presentations with specific attention to group presentations, questions and answers, meetings, and interviews. Each chapter includes specific suggestions on the types of presentations we are expected to give.

The book is tied together by a glossary of grammar, usage, logic and organization, format, spelling, and punctuation. End-of-chapter questions and an appendix with workshop exercises provide a model for instruction that can be applied to full courses or to short seminars.

This book recognizes that we have all had some experience in writing or speaking. The initial lessons of composition and communication were taught in "grammar" school, and although these lessons may have been incomplete or forgotten, we still manage to perform the daily "business" of communication. Nevertheless, now we must remember what we once learned and apply that knowledge to our specific needs. We need to understand how to revise, how to improve, how to be more concise, how to persuade, and how to evaluate the quality of our communication.

In writing or speaking, we follow the same rules of language and logic. These rules for clear communication apply to all disciplines. Business writing and speaking, technical writing, legal writing, or academic writing require no special variations. The differences lie in tone and in the types of words used in a specific profession. In short, variations of style among professional disciplines depend on the established audience.

The reason for joining writing and speaking in the same book seems clear: speakers and writers have to know how to put ideas together into meaningful sentences. In other words, clear writing precedes effective speaking. To do both, we must know the subject well and understand the audience's needs. We should know the function of grammar and syntax, the precise meanings of words, and the ways to develop clear arguments. The rules that underlie writing also enable us to speak clearly.

What will be the use of our communication? Certainly immortality is not the goal of the professional world; in fact, only a tiny percentage of the words we speak or write are immortalized. Instead, we normally communicate to inform or persuade, to create the understanding that leads to cooperation. For these purposes, clarity and grace in language can lead to successful communication. After all, people are judged by their words as well as their actions.

Over the years, many people have tried to impart to me the valuable lessons of grace and precision. I am especially grateful to former teachers: Thomas Gilligan, who taught discipline in writing; William Koerber, who taught the power of words; and Keith Lindblom, friend and mentor, who taught the importance of making sense. I wish to acknowledge the guidance of the late J. Crozier Schaefer, who sought only one thing: perfection. He demanded it of himself and hoped for it in others. For enabling me to take the time to begin this book, I would like to thank Donald C. Carroll, former dean of the Wharton School of the University of Pennsylvania.

My wife Wendy has been steadfast in her support. She has made incisive comments on the manuscript and has patiently discussed the various transformations from first to last draft. My daughter Elizabeth has also helped me to understand that words should solve problems and not raise them.

My brother Martin, writer and editor, is a teacher's teacher. He has taught me to search for ambiguity and wordiness.

Other friends and colleagues have offered helpful suggestions. My thanks to Richard A. Block, Ann Bohara, Rosalind Carter, John Gaggin, Anne Greenhalgh, and David Wolford. I am also grateful to others who have made valuable comments on the manuscript: Paul Anderson, Miami University, Ohio; Paul A. Argenti, Amos Tuck School of Business, Dartmouth College; Alan T. Belsches, University of North Carolina; Vincent DiSalvo, University of Nebraska; Robert Gieselman, University of Illinois; Carolyn Gold, Marshalls, Inc.; Barbara Jensen-Osinski, Rauch Center for Executive Development, Lehigh University; James J. Kiely, Bentley College; Robert E. Reinheimer, Fuqua School of Business, Duke University; Kathryn J. Seidel, University of Maryland; Gary Shaw, Colgate Darden School of Business, University of Virginia; John W. Simms, AT&T Bell Laboratories; and Betty Evans White, Washington University.

A short time ago, I told my colleague, Roland M. Frye, a distinguished professor of Renaissance studies, that while preparing this book I was learning how to write again. He asked me how old I was, and when I answered, he said, "You have about eleven more times left." Learning to communicate is a lifetime process.

Larry M. Robbins

The Business of Writing and Speaking

A Managerial Communication Manual

PART 1

General Principles of Composition

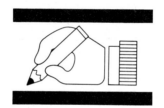

Chapter 1

The Nature and Uses of Communication

The Process of Communication

The prefix of the word *process—pro*—denotes forward movement; the whole word denotes the idea of change. Communication creates change because the participants in the exchange of ideas learn something that adds to their store of knowledge. Since not all communication is effective, not all change is positive. When communication is clear and logical, the barriers to change are removed and the process of increasing knowledge or motivating someone to act moves forward.

Communication is a process involving a sender and a receiver. The writer or speaker sends a message which is supposed to elicit a response from a listener or speaker. Thus, communication is a two-way process. Poor communication occurs when the line is broken between sender and receiver or between receiver and sender. The interruption or "noise" preventing clear communication can be faulty organization or misinformation on the sender's part or the receiver's inability to understand or listen to the message.

The message directed to a particular audience is a primary form of communication. Often, however, the sender will reach a secondary audience of

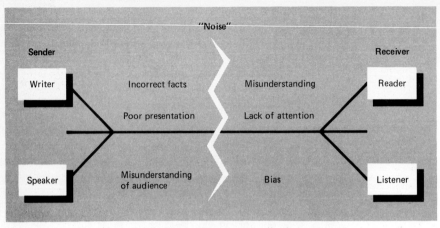

Figure 1-1   Interrupting the communication process

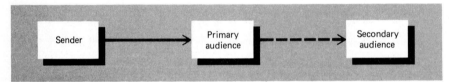

Figure 1-2   Primary and secondary audiences

receivers (readers or listeners). For example, a memo written by a company's research director to project heads may eventually be read by the comptroller or a lawyer. Therefore, the writer should avoid the use of jargon, vague allusions, and confusing abbreviations. In one firm, the abbreviation M & E had two meanings. The accountants thought that it meant *maintenance and equipment*, while the engineering department defined M & E as *mechanics and engineering*. Writers and speakers can avoid costly confusion if they ask themselves, "Would someone with a limited knowledge of my topic understand what I am saying?" The secondary audience may be peripheral, but they may need to respond to communication between the sender and the primary audience. For example, a memo concerning safety regulations may be sent to department heads, but the memo also may be posted for all employees. To respond sensibly, the secondary audience must be able to understand the communication.

Levels of Communication

Whether you are communicating to a group or to an individual, you need to plan carefully to meet the audience's needs. In interpersonal communication, the sender can analyze the audience of one and design the message to meet very specific needs. If the message is not completely clear, the receiver can ask a question that will clear up uncertainty. In group communication, the sender must try to avoid every ambiguity because all the members of the audience will not be able to respond personally. In either type of communication, the speaker or writer must anticipate the audience's response and use facts and logic to prevent ambiguity.

INTERPERSONAL COMMUNICATION

People may talk to themselves or imagine conversations, but as Paul R. Timm has said, "such internal communication is another way to describe thinking."[1] Interpersonal communication occurs when an individual has direct interaction with every member of an "audience." The audience may be one other person, or it may be a group in which people interact with one another. Communication between individuals requires the skills of organization, clear expression, and listening.

Organizing.   Since interpersonal communication involves reacting as well as initiating, you cannot control all interactions between people. Nevertheless, keeping the purpose of the discussion in mind will guide you to your goal. In a business setting, which may extend from an office interview to cocktail conversation, two people may wish to discuss a problem as equals, or one person may wish to establish authority. For example, a superior usually leads a conversation by introducing new topics, asking pertinent questions, and stating conclusions. Subordinates may wish to show deference to the superior by following the superior's lead, or they may wish to establish their own credibility by responding accurately and by directing the discussion according to their own personal agenda. In the give and take of communication, participants should defer to the common goal, if there is one; or, at least, they should be willing to listen as well as talk. *Planning* helps attain the flexibility needed to achieve the goals of a particular type of communication.

Expressing ideas clearly.   In conversations or official meetings between two people, participants should have a goal in mind in order to eliminate digressions and ambiguity. Many people begin sentences two or three times before coming to the point; others start a sentence without knowing how to conclude. To avoid misunderstanding, write out a simple outline before the conversation begins or make a mental outline as the meeting progresses. Try to use simple sentence structure and unpretentious words. When making a statement, eliminate the digressive preface (I'm not sure whether I should ask this or not, but . . . .") and come to the point. When answering a question, give a complete but simple answer, and once you have answered the question, do not repeat yourself or

---

[1] *Managerial Communication* (Englewood Cliffs, N.J.: Prentice-Hall, 1980), p. 16.

digress to other ideas. As successful salespeople have learned, knowing when to stop talking is an important skill.

Listening.   Effective communication of any type—but especially interpersonal communication where immediate response is demanded—requires careful listening. To be a good listener, you must maintain eye contact, just as a speaker must. By looking directly at a person, you prevent yourself from being distracted, and in turn you make the speaker concentrate on you. As you listen, you can make mental notes of the main points the speaker covers and of the questions you wish to ask in response. Receptive listeners can facilitate communication by responding with a nod or facial expression. A positive nod gives the speaker confidence to continue; a negative or quizzical look causes the speaker to clarify ideas immediately. The interaction between a well-organized speaker and a receptive listener leads to successful communication because both participants have anticipated and responded to each other's needs.

GROUP COMMUNICATION

Communication by an individual to a group requires all the skills of interpersonal communication—planning, assessing audience needs, flexibility, clarity of expression, etc. The main difference between interpersonal and group communication is that a group cannot provide an immediate and uniform verbal response. Since most (but certainly not all) presentations to a group do not allow interruptions, the speaker must assume that if a message is well-prepared, the audience is receiving it clearly.

In memos and letters, try to remove ambiguity by planning and revision. When writing memos to more than one person, assume that your audience has a common level of knowledge about a topic and a common need to be informed or persuaded. After establishing purpose and audience needs, you should order facts in a logical sequence that will help achieve the objective of the communication. Breakdowns in communication occur when the sender fails to reach a common level of understanding with the audience or when the receiver lets personal bias distort the listening process that leads to understanding.

Tools of Communication

LANGUAGE AND GRAMMAR

Every language has developed standards in its evolution, for without rules of syntax, ambiguity would make language useless. The English language evolved from Germanic roots with many infusions of Latin and French words. Usage became codified, and today there exists a tongue called Received Standard

English, used mostly (if at all) by graduates of Cambridge and Oxford.[2] Even the *name* of this kind of English suggests a divine giver of language who thunders at "mistakes."

The argument between those who prescribe rules and those who describe usage need not be resolved, *except* by an individual writer or speaker. A writer must make decisions about audience, tone, and diction (types of words) in order to use language effectively. There are times when "Quiet!" is far more effective than "Silence is requested."

Before you can decide which rules to follow, you must know those rules. Words convey meaning, but if the words appear randomly, no one can understand them: "Closed collapsed building today the because the stock market." Thus, for the sake of survival, we learn grammar and syntax when we start speaking in whole sentences. That is, we learn what forms are *proper* without knowing their names. Knowing the names of grammatical forms is unnecessary if words are to be spoken once and forgotten, but writers who want their words to be durable need to understand the tools of language (grammar, syntax, structure) in order to revise and improve. Only conscientious revision can lead to clarity, and that process requires knowing what it means to change the passive voice to the active, to eliminate prepositional phrases, or to use the restrictive or the nonrestrictive pronoun consistently. Is it a hard job to remember all the grammar learned (or not learned) in school? Not really. Only a basic grammar review is necessary and a willingness to examine each word, phrase, or clause to see what works and what fails.

LOGIC AND ORGANIZATION

Failures in communication are part of life, unfortunately. Even the most precise words, in the best English, may cause confusion if logic is lacking. Therefore, it is essential to test logic before presenting ideas to the public. This topic will be discussed more fully in Chapter 3, but as you begin to think about the process of communication, consider the following ways to test the logical validity of your statements.

For deductive logic, use the "how?" and "why?" test. After every sentence, ask "how?" or "why?" to see if you have supported your statements. The answer to "how?" is "by means of," and the answer to "why?" is "because." *Because* clarifies, because all the steps of logic are filled in—assertion, support, conclusion. In most cases, the answers to "how?" or "why?" will be in the sentence itself or in the very next sentence. If the answers are lacking, *by means of* and *because* will supply the supporting ideas needed to compose a coherent paragraph.

---

[2]See "Received Standard English" and "Received Pronunciation," *The American Heritage Dictionary,* 2d college ed. (Boston: Houghton Mifflin, 1982).

STATEMENT NEEDING SUPPORT

"The government ought to prevent the bankruptcy of corporations essential to the national welfare." How? " . . . *by granting emergency loans.*" Why? " . . . *to prevent a serious disruption of the national economy.*"

STATEMENT COMPLETE IN ITSELF

"To prevent a serious disruption of the national economy (*why*), the government ought to prevent the bankruptcy of corporations essential to the national welfare by granting emergency loans (*how*)."

Logic, syntax, and grammar are not the only tools needed for clear communication. Without tight organization, overall meaning may be lost in random thoughts. There are many ways to organize ideas: by time sequence, by place, or by natural relationships (comparison and contrast, cause and effect). Whatever method you use, another simple test will help keep the organization in order. At the left-hand margin of every paragraph, write down a capital letter (A, B, C, etc.). At major divisions, insert a roman numeral. This outline *after the fact* should correspond to the outline made before any words were set down. If the two outlines are not the same, there is nothing to worry about. The second one will probably reflect sensible revisions of organization. Compare both to see if you have conveyed all relevant points in a logical order.

REVISION

By now it should be clear that effective communication requires planning, organizing, and revising. However, many beleaguered writers and speakers say, "If I spend all my time revising, I'll never get anything done. And besides, I barely have time to finish a first draft before it's due." Revision can speed up communication, not slow it down. If you know you use too many prepositional phrases ("*available to the organization to the fullest extent*") or too many compounds ("*significant and important*"), you can eliminate this "clutter"[3] as you write, saving time for the more important change in logic and organization.

Experienced writers know that they can improve a manuscript by eliminating excess words, correcting minor errors, adding a supporting argument, or rearranging paragraphs for the sake of coherence. Eventually, writers can learn to make such changes as they write if they know the simple rules of revision. (See Chapter 4 for a discussion of the process of revision.)

The process of revision should be applied to writing and speaking alike. Is the diction consistent? Is the style polysyllabic or simple, stiff, or colloquial? Good writers and speakers keep their audiences in mind at all times, being neither pretentious nor patronizing. What people say should always be more important

---

[1]A term used by William Zinsser, *On Writing Well,* 2d ed. (New York: Harper & Row, 1980), p. 14.

than how they say it, and if language is filled with confusing noun strings ("officer analyst interaction system") or awful metaphors ("run it up the flagpole to get a better bottom line") then meaning may be lost in a muddle of words.

Careful revision should result in achieving the purpose of the communication. If the purpose is to inform, then the reader should learn something valuable. If the purpose is to persuade, the audience should be motivated by fact and logic to take action.

Barriers to Communication

PERSONAL BARRIERS

For some people, the process of communication is so intimidating that "writer's block" or stage fright creates an almost insurmountable barrier. For others, not knowing what to say or how to say it results in the surmountable problem of procrastination. And for everyone, being anxious about the effect of words on an audience can establish still another barrier. Understanding the reasons for these barriers, some of them self-imposed, may help eliminate them.

Writer's block. Inadequate information is the first symptom of writer's block. Some writers are afraid to face the blank page because they think they do not know enough about the subject. This problem occurs when the process begins in the middle, namely, when writing begins before research and organization have taken place. Even writing down a title or topic will help focus ideas. After choosing a topic, write down a thesis statement or one-sentence abstract of your objective. Then write a simple sentence outline, covering major categories and subcategories. Expand that outline into a topic outline with key words and phrases you can use in the text. Fill in the outline with facts, and *then* you are ready to write.

A second symptom of writer's block is a feeling of inadequacy. By not knowing how to edit and revise your own writing, you lose control over your words. You submit a draft to a superior or editor, and the manuscript is returned with red-ink tamperings that look like your own blood. True, some editors are autocrats and will put back mistakes you have corrected or replace your ideas with their own. However, because of their experience and acute sense of audience, good editors will exercise just enough authority to make your manuscript represent the organization. If editors are sensitive, they will improve the product without defacing the writer's personality.

After the months or years it takes to serve an apprenticeship and learn your job, you can gain your own authorial voice. Credibility and self-confidence result from presenting consistently accurate information and valid arguments. The fantasy of believing that someday everything (or even something) you write will be returned with no red ink may never come true because you will still need to adhere to *house style* or editorial policy. However, if you are not afraid of the editing process, and if you do some of it yourself, you will remove one of the barriers causing writer's block—intimidation.

Writer's block has many causes: lack of information, poor organization, faulty logic, incorrect usage, and the fear of disapproval. You can begin to eliminate these problems by carefully analyzing some of your own writing and the writing of others. Find the mistakes, and try to avoid them the next time you write. A blank page does not have to be intimidating if you understand that writing requires planning and revision.

Stage fright.   If writer's block is intimidating, stage fright is terrifying—at least to speakers who concentrate on themselves instead of their audiences. A certain amount of apprehension is positive because it will cause you to prepare as well as you can. Good preparation, which includes analyzing the audience's needs, organizing logically, and rehearsing, will eliminate most of the fear of the unknown. While speaking, good eye contact and attention to body movement will help establish communication between you and the audience. You will not be hurling ideas to the general mass but presenting your facts to individuals. No one can, or probably should, be able to eliminate apprehension completely. However, there is no reason to let fear of speaking block professional advancement. The chapters of this book on oral communication will present some suggestions on controlling a fear stronger than the fear of heights or heart attacks.

ORGANIZATIONAL BARRIERS

The personal barriers of writer's block and stage fright can be overcome by experience. Often, though, even the best writers and speakers will face barriers having nothing to do with communication skills. A memo to a subordinate may be clear, but if the subordinate is not motivated to action, the communication fails. Sometimes the communications of superiors are not clear, and the subordinate cannot act without asking for clarification. Or, vague ethical standards may block effective communication because the reader has to infer the truth. No clear communication has ever been written between the lines.

Barriers between superiors and subordinates.   Superiors are responsible for implementing company policy, but they should not let their authority make them dictators of style. In a large financial organization which publishes a quarterly journal, the supervisor was dissatisfied with the quality of writing sent to him for editing, and the employees were unhappy with what seemed to be arbitrary changes. To begin solving this problem, all staff members, including the supervising editor and his superior, attended a seminar to discuss ways to improve individual writing so that the copy was "cleaner" before being submitted to the editor. The editor, in turn, was able to give reasons why he had to make certain kinds of changes. He was more interested in testing logic and organization and removing wordiness than he was in changing meaning or imposing his own style. This editor removed a serious barrier to communication by *establishing* communication. He still had final authority, but he did not let anyone's personality dominate the published articles.

Barriers affecting subordinates.   Subordinates often react negatively to editing or suggestions for revision, especially when the boss "utilizes excessive obfuscatory locutions" instead of using simple language. Rather than being angry at editorial changes, subordinates should evaluate their own style and the superior's changes. Perhaps the boss is right. After all, superiors have experience in their profession and have established a sense of company policy and company needs that relatively inexperienced employees have not yet acquired. Whether or not the boss is right, the employee must work within the system while maintaining integrity. In matters of content and audience, the superior should have the final authority. In matters of grammar and usage, style books can supply the authority and can be used as support. In matters of fact, the original writer has the ultimate responsibility. The best way, then, to approach the problem of communication block from above is to provide the kinds of facts and logic that will enable superiors to exercise their editorial judgment for the sake of the organization's goals.

Barriers between peers.   Another barrier to communication often exists between coworkers. For example, many offices have a "mad memo writer" who wants to demonstrate a high level of activity and self-importance. This person may also talk too much. As in any type of communication, if you have something important to say—say it; if communication is for self-aggrandizement, you will lose the cooperation of colleagues who believe that completing a job is more important than talking about it.

Ethics and law.   A serious barrier to communication is caused by vague ethical standards. Many will argue that it is sometimes unnecessary or even damaging to say everything; however, incomplete information at best causes confusion and at worst is deceptive.

The legal system in the United States has helped establish and maintain ethical standards. Since laws govern actions, especially where contracts are involved, everything that becomes part of the public record—written or spoken—must be able to withstand legal inquiry. Memos written for the record, sales proposals and agreements, reports and presentations not only must be unambiguous, they must be accurate. Sometimes the final audience of a communication can be a judge or jury; if we all communicate with the idea that we are responsible legally for our words, then we will anticipate the problems caused by incomplete or inaccurate information. We should not be intimidated, just responsible, professional, and careful.

The Function of Communication

Communication is a continuing process; it does not end when a message is sent or when it is received. Individual messages—speeches, memos, meetings—form part of a system of communication between individuals and among groups. If the communication is clear from the outset, then both the receiver and the sender will have achieved their goal—understanding of information.

ORGANIZING

Gathering the facts needed for an effective memo or presentation will help you order your ideas into categories, and the categories should represent the way you handle your daily activities. In short, you need to know where to find technical data, past activities, financial information, etc. If your mind, file, and office are well-organized, this information will be easy to find. Preparing to communicate will help put things in order.

IMPLEMENTING

Informative communications make a statement of fact. Persuasive communications move the receiver to act. To motivate others successfully, you must present reasons and visualize the desired effect of your communication. Even if the reader has no choice but to accept your proposal or directive, the reason for action should be clear. If the only reason for acting is the company's welfare, both the receiver and the sender should know why an action is good for the company. Logic motivates.

The most important function of communication is to implement ideas. Thinking and research may develop a new product, but only working with others will help produce it. To work well with others you must be able to communicate ideas so that others understand you and do what you ask. Clear and concise communication translates thinking into action.

SUCCEEDING

In an essay on the attributes of success, Francis Bacon said, "Reading maketh a free man; conference a ready man; and writing an exact man."[4] In the twentieth

---

[4] "Of Studies," 1597.

century, John Fielden believes that this lesson, although neglected, needs to be learned again. In his essay, "What Do You Mean I Can't Write?" Fielden rates the ability to communicate as the prime characteristic of a promotable executive.[5]

Today, communication skills are not only requisites for promotion, they are needed for survival. An individual who communicates well has a better chance for survival and for increased productivity.

Individuals who improve their communication skills will increase the productivity of the organization. Since the number of memos written is not an accurate gauge of productivity, learning to write faster is not an important goal. Learning to communicate concisely is. Unimportant or inaccurate memos waste the time of writer and reader; well-planned presentations—oral or written— improve the ability to understand and the desire to act. In clear communications, the worn-out statement, "If you have any questions, please call me," should not be necessary because the questions have been answered. If the reader wishes to respond, then communication moves forward to an extension or application of the ideas and not backward to an explanation. Productivity decreases when individuals have to go back to find out what went wrong.

Quality improves when communication is exact. Bacon said that "conference" makes a ready man (today we can read "manager") and writing an exact man. To confer is to communicate, and to communicate successfully, you must be prepared with facts, logic, clarity, perception, anticipation, comprehension. Exactness means removing the clutter from ideas and expression. If your reader or listener says, "I understand what you say, I believe what you say, and I will do what you say," then your process of communication and its result will have been successful.

Exercises

1 Make a list of your personal barriers to communication. Divide the list into:
   a internal barriers
   b external barriers

2 Identify the primary audiences with whom you usually communicate. Identify the secondary audiences who are usually peripheral to your communication. Do the two types of audiences ever overlap?

3 Review the last manuscript you wrote. Circle known errors and possible errors.

4 Review the last memo or letter you received. Determine overall organization, look for obvious errors, and write down a very brief synopsis of the meaning. What was the communication supposed to achieve? Did it achieve its goal?

---

[5] *Harvard Business Review* (May-June 1964), p. 1.

Chapter 2

Purpose, Audience, and Preparation

Determining Purpose

Why write? Why speak? Because you have something important to say or because you are assigned the task of communicating ideas. Before beginning any formal communication, you must determine your purpose. In the context of business, the two most useful types of communication are information and persuasion. Of course, these two functions are closely related. A successful persuasive communication must be based on sound information, and an informative document can persuade a reader to believe you if the facts are complete and presented logically.

INFORMATION

If conveying information is your main reason for writing, first determine the kind of facts you need to communicate. Shorter forms of informative writing include announcements, policy statements, new procedures, trip or meeting reports, and periodic reviews. These tasks will require you to concentrate on accuracy and completeness. For example, in a meeting announcement, always include date, time, place, and agenda. For all short informative writing you will need to gather and verify relevant facts: times, places, people involved, sequence of events, financial data, or any other information that will make your communication complete.

Detailed research belongs in longer reports whose format requires background, methodology, analysis, and supporting tables or illustrations. For longer informative communications, an abstract or summary will direct the reader to the conclusions developed within the entire document. No matter how much information you wish to convey, keep the organization clear and the style simple. Just give the facts in a logical sequence.

SAMPLE INFORMATIVE MEMO

TO: All Department Heads

FROM: E. C. Nelson
                Vice President, Personnel

SUBJECT: Staggered Working Hours

DATE: June 1, 19--

The executive committee[1] has passed a resolution authorizing staggered working hours for all employees.[2] Please establish a schedule for your department and send a copy to me.[3] The new work schedule will begin July 1, 19--.[4]

---

[1] Actor.
[2] Action taken.
[3] Action required of receiver.
[4] Date of implementation.

This sequence contains basic elements of information: *who, what,* and *when.* The *who* is divided into those who have taken action and those who need to take action. The memo might have included a reason for taking action ("to reduce traffic congestion" or "to enable all employees to arrive at work on time"), but in simple directives like this one the rationale for action may raise irrelevant policy issues.

PERSUASION

Persuasive writing requires credible information and sound logic. If you want your reader to take action, you will have to provide enough information for a decision, and you will have to appeal to reason or emotion (or both). Consider the following elements of a persuasive appeal: Begin by establishing the problem to be solved, including facts that demonstrate the seriousness of the issue. Involve the audience by showing how the problem affects them. Establish criteria for solving the problem and then present possible solutions. After a *brief* review of other solutions, offer your own and support it with fact and logic. Conclude with a specific recommendation and the visualization of a successful resolution to the problem if your recommendation is accepted. If you appeal to emotion or logic, provide factual support for your proposal, and offer a successful solution to a problem, you will have brought your audience to the point of decision.

SAMPLE PERSUASIVE MEMO

TO: Executive Committee

FROM: Evelyn Allen
Head, Plant Development Committee

SUBJECT: Addition to Existing Plant

DATE: March 1, 19--

As we all know, our chief competitor opened a new plant last June, and by the end of the year, they surpassed us in sales.[1] The executive committee must find a way to improve our sales and regain leadership in the industry.[2]

Responding to the competition and to our own development goals, the executive committee has asked for a proposal to expand production capabilities.[3] In the past three months, the plant development committee has surveyed seven potential building sites and has completed a feasibility study for an addition to our existing facilities. Although a new plant would be 15% larger than an addition, savings in land, construction, and relocation costs will offset the slightly greater capacity of a new facility.[4] With an addi-

> tion to existing facilities, production could be integrated in order to make up the difference in capacity offered by a new facility built at some distance from our headquarters.[5]
>
> Please review the attached financial data showing comparative costs of the addition and a new plant. I recommend that you approve this proposal at the next board meeting.[6] If you act immediately, we can start construction in the next quarter and begin to challenge our competitor by the end of next year.[7]

[1]Problem to be solved.
[2]Personal involvement.
[3]Criteria for solution.
[4]Possible solutions.
[5]Preferred solution.
[6]Recommendation.
[7]Visualization of success.

This memo contains only the basic facts and arguments; financial details and construction plans would appear in an appendix. To persuade the reader to act, the memo concentrates on personal involvement, the need to make a decision, and the prospect for success.

Defining Topic

After determining the purpose of a communication, you will need to define and limit your topic. For those who experience "writer's block," knowing how to select a topic may help solve the problem of starting to write. Many reports and memos cover too much. Instead of writing about all of the company's research and development projects or wasting time with a general historical review, restrict the topic by adding a limiting or defining term: research and development of a *new eye medicine;* computer techniques *in the accounting department.*

Once you have limited the topic, you can begin determining the subcategories needed to support your main ideas. For example, if as a consultant or student, you are writing about new developments in real estate loans, you may wish to select a specific type of loan (variable rate mortgage) and present a thorough history and analysis of the topic. Your supporting data will be easier to gather because you do not have to learn about the entire field of real estate investment. You will have moved from the general category of investment to progressively more specific categories: investment, real estate loans, variable rate mortgages. By being specific, you will simplify the task of finding the right information and eliminating the irrelevant. Even if your task is to write a complete report on a general field, defining and staying with subtopics will make the task of writing each section more manageable.

Research

As you investigate your topic, you can determine what is relevant if you always keep your main purpose in mind. Exhaustive research of an entire field is not necessary before you begin writing because in most cases you will be familiar with the general background. Certainly, demonstrating an understanding of overall issues will help you achieve credibility, but you do not need to read every book or article on the theory of investment before writing about a specific type of real estate venture. If your purpose remains clear, you will be able to divide your findings into three categories: applicable to the topic, related, and unrelated.

To begin your research, use the expanding resources of a college, public, or mercantile library. Reference librarians will direct you to the printed bibliographies and indexes applicable to your topic. Start with printed sources because you can focus on a specific topic by seeing what information is immediately available.

The computer has become a useful tool in research because it stores, organizes, and recalls vast amounts of information. Many libraries can help you complete a computerized literature search of the databanks available in major fields of inquiry—business, social sciences, science, and humanities. Most searches will be in bibliographic databases which contain citations to articles, books, and reports; some of these databases will also provide abstracts. Other databases are "nonbibliographic" and contain statistics, directory information, news reports, descriptions of organizations, and reports on research in progress. To find out what database seems most appropriate, consult such publications as *Computer-Readable Databases: A Directory and Data Sourcebook*[1] and *Directory of Online Information Resources.*[2] In the area of business, one of the *many* databases is *Management Contents,*[3] which provides current information in the areas of accounting, decision sciences, finance, marketing, etc., from 500 periodicals, proceedings, and books. This database is accompanied by a publication entitled *Management Contents Data Base Thesaurus,*[4] containing key words and the number of times the words appear in the database.

To initiate a search, select a term: e.g., *variable rate mortgage.* This term

[1]Urbana, IL: American Society for Information Science, 1982.
[2]Kensington, MD: CSG Press, 1983.
[3]Northbrook, IL: Management Contents, Inc., 1974.
[4]Northbrook, IL: Management Contents, Inc., 1981.

contains the general subject, *mortgage*, and the related key words, *variable rate*. After consulting the *Data Base Thesaurus*, enter the subject and key words into the computer, and the terminal will display the number of items containing these words. You can then ask for a sample of a few entries, perhaps five or so. If most are not applicable, ask for another sample. A "hit ratio" of relevant entries of about 50 percent will warrant completion of the search. Even fewer might be worthwhile if the items focus on your topic. After reading the titles and (if available) the abstracts, you can decide to complete the search and order an off-line printout to be mailed from the database's source. The costs of bibliographic searching vary according to vendor and are usually based on usage per minute. An average search will cost about $25 to $40 for 100 entries. These figures represent library costs; many databases are now being made available to personal computers, providing instant information at home or in the office.

STEPS IN A COMPUTER SEARCH

Step 1   Select term: *variable rate mortgage.*

Step 2   Consult a bibliography of databases: *Computer-Readable Databases: A Directory and Data Sourcebook.*

Step 3   Determine appropriate database: *Management Contents.*

Step 4   Consult a database thesaurus for key words: *Management Contents Data Base Thesaurus.*

Step 5   Begin on-line search by entering subject: *Mortgage* and key words: *variable rate, adjustable rate, fixed rate.* Computer will display number of relevant items as follows:

```
*SIGN-ON   13.49.01              09/23/83:

BRS/MGMT/1974 - AUG 1983

BRS - SEARCH MODE  - ENTER QUERY
    1_:    mortgage.de.

   RESULT     1026

    2_:   variable adj rate$1

   RESULT      109

    3_:   adjustable adj rate$1

   RESULT       23

    4_:    2 or 3

   RESULT      130

    5_:   fixed adj rate$1

   RESULT      143

    6_:    4 or 5
```

```
RESULT       252

7_:     1 and 6

RESULT       91

8_:     1 and 2

RESULT       49

9_:     ..p 8 ti/doc=1-3


    1
TI Selection of an index for Variable Rate Mortgages.


    2
TI Alternate Rate Mortgages: A Must for the 1980's.


    3
TI A Simple Model of Variable-Rate Mortgages.

              END OF DOCUMENTS
```

Step 6 Call up samples of titles alone or titles with abstracts:

```
:      ..p 8 all/doc=2

    2
AN BAK81D0098. 8302
AU Dodson, J.C..
TI Alternate Rate Mortgages: A Must for the 1980's.
SO ABA Banking Journal, Vol.73, No.4, April 1981, P. 98-100.
CD BAK..
YR 81..
DE Banks-and-Banking; Mortgage; Lending; Analysis.
AB The traditional long-term, fixed-rate mortgage is being found to be
   no longer viable.  The renegotiable rate mortgages are long-term
   mortgages with terms that can be changed every three to five years.
   Graduated payment mortgages start at a lower level for monthly
   payment and gradually increase.  Variable rate mortgages can be
   changed monthly and are therefore unstable.  Reverse annuity
   mortgages, shared appreciation mortgages, and deferred interest
   loans are other plans that are available.  The renegotiable rate
   mortgage is probably the one that will best meet the needs of the
   future.
PT Journal.
              END OF DOCUMENT
```

Step 7 Complete search. For shorter searches (up to 50 items), print on-line results immediately. For longer searches, off-line printouts can be cheaper because actual computer time is restricted to sampling.

After initial research into a library's printed sources, you should be able to settle on your topic. When you have decided to discuss the specific issue of variable rate mortgages instead of the general topic of *loans*, you can complete a computer search to help identify relevant information. No matter how you search for supporting material, throughout your planning and preparation you will have to continue asking how much and what kind of additional support you will need. Primary sources (individual experiments, published or unpublished speeches, letters, historical records, conversations, and interviews) added to secondary sources (published material such as books, journals, documents, and atlases) will provide the authoritative background you will need in order to be credible and persuasive. Often, research continues while you write, but once you have enough supporting data to make a case, you can start organizing your research into a logical outline.

Outlining

Every communication should have a plan that develops logic and balance of ideas. If you wish to inform, persuade, demonstrate, announce, or denounce, know your conclusion in advance. This principle applies to writing and speaking alike. There are many ways to organize, but whatever method you choose always make an outline as a guide. Although you may deviate from the outline while writing, at least your deviations will not be random.

TYPES OF OUTLINES

Simple outline.   The simple outline is a brief, one- or two-word list of major topics.

DESCRIPTION OF A LITERATURE SEARCH

1. Term

2. Database bibliography

3. Appropriate database

4. Thesaurus

5. Key words

6. Sample of relevant items

7. Search and printout

This type of outline helps you order sequences or ideas. The simple outline makes it possible to analyze the logic of the overall organization. Once the main topics appear in the correct order, it is easier to expand the outline into subcategories.

Sentence outline.   Some people like to write out complete thoughts in sentence form. This can be a tedious process, but it can help you break down the barrier called writer's block. After a few sentences written in a logical sequence, the blank page begins to yield ideas that can be expanded into paragraphs. The following outline on the audit process shows how explanations in conversational sentences help put ideas into words.

THE AUDIT PROCESS

I. Contact the client to arrange a meeting.
  A. Make sure all pertinent documents are available.
  B. Make sure the people responsible for keeping the books and making decisions will be available.

II. Complete the audit.
  A. Check over the balance sheets, verifying each entry with the appropriate documents.
  B. Look for places where information may be incomplete.
  C. Double-check every total.

III. Meet with the client.
  A. Show how the conclusions were reached.
  B. Ask if the client has additional information or questions.
  C. Have the client agree to the conclusions.
  D. If the client won't agree, prepare a qualified opinion.

The sentence outline contains complete thoughts but without reasons or transitions between sentences or categories. Many times, sentences written as part of an outline can be transferred directly to the final draft.

Topic outline.   In a topic outline, headline form is used, eliminating the need to write everything out. The visual format of a topic outline enables the writer to balance categories and subcategories according to their importance.

Begin the topic outline, like the simple outline, by listing major categories, using roman numerals. Then add subtopics in descending order of importance, remembering that each category must have at least two entries to show balance, comparison, or contrast. Thus, every I has to have a II, and every *A* has to have a *B*, etc. You will probably not need to go beyond five subcategories. Each subcategory should be balanced with the kind and amount of material necessary for logical support. Do not make the outline so complex that subcategories outweigh major categories. Should this happen, rethink the outline, making new major categories and deleting irrelevant subcategories.

OUTLINE FORMAT

I.
  A.
  B.
      1.
          a.
          b.
              (1)
              (2)
      2.
  C.
II.

Use roman numerals to introduce major categories, capital letters to introduce first subcategories, and arabic numerals and lowercase letters for categories of increasing complexity and decreasing importance. Use numbers and then letters enclosed in parentheses to give specific details.

Proper spacing helps in visualizing the size and importance of categories. For horizontal spacing, clear for the longest roman numeral (such as III or VIII) so that the periods will align. Allow four spaces for all other letters or numbers. For vertical spacing, double-space between roman numerals and capital letters, and single-space between arabic numerals and lowercase letters.

Capital letters show the progression from major categories to subcategories. Capitalize the first letter of all main words in a major category and first subcategory, capitalize the first letter only of the second subcategory and use lowercase for all words in other subcategories.

ILLUSTRATION: PARTIAL ROMAN NUMERAL TOPIC OUTLINE
THE CONSULTING PROCESS

I.   Investigate Client Organization

II.   Agree on Project

III.   Plan Project
    A.   Goals
        1.   Client
        2.   Consultant
    B.   Scope
        1.   Main issue
        2.   Related issues
    C.   Information Needed
        1.   Statistical
            a.   market surveys
            b.   demographic data
                (1)   national
                (2)   regional
                    (*a*)   metropolitan area
                    (*b*)   neighborhoods
        2.   Financial

IV.   Implement Project

In addition to consistent spacing, numbering, and capitalizing, grammatical consistency helps to place ideas in a logical order. As in any list, each entry should begin with the same part of speech: usually a noun, gerund, or verb. In a topic outline, use headline form, eliminating articles and punctuation.

The roman numeral outline provides a logical sequence of major categories, subcategories, and specific examples. The same sequence can be achieved in an exclusively arabic numbering system found in many technical reports. Each entry in the outline will usually correspond to a complete paragraph in the text.

PARTIAL ARABIC NUMERAL TOPIC OUTLINE

PERSONNEL MANUAL

1.   Personnel Procedures for New Employees

   1.1.   Hiring

   1.2.   Job evaluation

      1.2.1.   Observation by supervisor

      1.2.2.   Interview with employee

2.   Personnel Procedures for Current Employees

Regardless of the numbering system, if you take the time to make an effective outline, you will have a clear guide for writing and a checklist to apply after you complete the first draft. If the draft does not exactly correspond to the outline, make a new outline so that you can check the completed document against the plan. Good communication should be well planned but with room for spontaneity.

Determining Audience

After determining the purpose and plan of your communication, you should begin analyzing your audience. Ask three questions: Who are they? What do they want to know? What do you want them to know? The answers are complex because if you do not know everyone personally, job titles may not tell you enough about the individual. For example, when speaking to members of an engineering firm do not assume that the audience will be engineers; they may all be accountants or from the purchasing department.

In establishing the audience, first assume that they need to be informed. They may have asked you for information, or you may have information that they need to know. Second, assume that the audience needs to act. Even in an informative memo or speech, the audience should learn something that will enable them to act because they will know more than they did before. Persuasive communications motivate an audience to change a situation as a result of the information and logic you have presented.

Before you begin writing, try to establish the audience's level of knowledge about the subject. Do they understand the general field, and would any of them have prior knowledge of your specific topic? If you do not know the primary receivers of your message, consult publicly accessible personnel records for company history, and ask one member of your potential audience to describe the needs of the group. Usually, you will not need to ask about personal idiosyncrasies, but knowing if the chairman of the board is color-blind will help you design visual aids.

A general assessment of the audience's knowledge will help determine how much or how little information you need to include. Most audiences will not mind listening to a brief review of general principles as a background to a specific application. By reviewing principles, you will establish common definitions, and then you can use the level of detail the audience will understand.

After establishing the audience's depth of knowledge, assess their attitude toward the subject. Will they be receptive or hostile, open-minded or inflexible? What facts do they need in order to advance their knowledge? What arguments will convince them that your way is best? Play devil's advocate and anticipate objections while establishing a common ground of agreement.

Audience Profile

Before beginning to write or speak, write down answers to specific questions about the audience. Consider the following list.

1   Who are they? Profession, title, level of responsibility, education, experience, age, prominent members?

2   What is your relationship to them? Employer, supervisor, teacher; peers with equal knowledge and responsibility; subordinate, employee, someone uninformed?

3   What is their general level of knowledge about the subject? Familiar, unfamiliar, peripheral?

4   What is their attitude toward the subject? Receptive, hostile, noncommittal, willing to be informed?

5   What are their expectations? To learn something, to make a decision, to act?

After you have answered these questions about your expected audience, offer them specific ideas and examples related to their own experience.

ATTITUDES TOWARD THE AUDIENCE

Honesty.   To establish credibility, the best way to approach an audience is with honesty. Have confidence in your own knowledge and ability to communicate simply. You do not need to use pretentious language to sound important, nor do you need to explain too much. If you have analyzed the audience carefully, you will not have to "talk down" by being superior or to impress by saying everything you know. If you are challenged, use logic to justify your assertions because sound logic, backed by fact, will make you believable. Keep your goal in mind at all times, and do not let wordiness or inappropriate tone cloud your message.

Deference.   At times, a humble tone, when matched with solid information, will break down an audience's negative attitude. For example, instead of telling executives what to do ("Get rid of the Acme division!"), give them facts and arguments that will enable them to make their own decisions. Effective writers approach their audience as equals, but they show respect for what individuals know and what they need to learn.

Level of knowledge.   The audience's level of knowledge about a subject will help you determine your attitude. When communicating to peers, assume that they share your knowledge and experience. They do not need to know general background. If the audience includes individuals with greater knowledge than yours, establish the general context to show you know the field ("court decisions of November and December, 19-- concerning mergers . . ."). Then move to the specific (". . . have opened the way for new talks with the Acme Corporation.") The board of directors should be familiar with the subject (mergers) and recent action (court decisions). They will want to hear what action you recommend.

If the audience has no knowledge of your topic, fill them in with brief statements of background and current situation. Specific facts will not offend any audience and will help you establish a common ground of understanding. Telling them too much (the meaning of *mergers*, all the laws dealing with mergers, 50 recent mergers) will bore them and divert you from your purpose of justifying company action. Telling them too little (leaving out previous attempts, new laws) will confuse them and not provide enough information to justify action.

Tone

APPROPRIATE TONE

The tone of letters or memos can be formal or informal, depending on purpose and audience. A colloquial tone can be inappropriate ("Your museum needs a promotional program that will give you more bang for your buck"), and an officious tone can offend or confuse ("Utilize our expertise to understand fully the virtues of our preowned vehicles.") In any communication, use words that explain, not hide. What you say should always be more important than how you say it.

Personal pronouns (I, you, we) show involvement; after all, letters are written by people, not by companies. To avoid emphasizing yourself, however, limit the personal pronoun, especially at the beginning of paragraphs. Choose a tone that supports the intent of the letter. Remember, too, when writing outside the United States, that most other cultures require formal distance and tone in correspondence.

TONING DOWN ANGER

While anger is an obvious tone, an angry communication is best torn up or toned down because venting anger may be only an emotional exercise. If you want to complain, always keep the purpose clear—send the check, stop unfair practices, clean up the neighborhood. Use tone to improve a situation, not to make it worse. The following letters show how emotion can be redirected toward solving a problem.

October 31, 19--

Dear Mr. Young:

It has come to my attention that you said I was undermining company policy. You have no right to misquote me about such a sensitive issue. I believe I gave all the details I needed to show how the company was lax. Since I did not see you in the audience, I am not sure you were even there. Your behavior is absolutely unacceptable, and I demand a formal retraction and an apology.

Yours truly,

Daniel Dryden

Although this letter is brief, the point it makes is not clear. The writer is apparently angry at a third-hand comment and without restating all the pertinent facts has let his emotions dominate: "you have no right," "absolutely unaccept-able," "demand." Because the issue is so personal and sensitive, a more objective response might solve the problem of misrepresentation. Waiting another day to write the letter will help the writer think more clearly.

November 1, 19--

Dear Bob,

I was distressed to hear that you misunderstood my position on company policy. At last Wednesday's meeting, I went over in detail the planning process that led to the recent decision for expansion. I believe I showed that an important step in the process was left out and that before any further action is taken, we should have all the facts.

I am sorry that you thought this criticism was negative. We ought to meet privately to discuss my objections and your apparent reaction. For the sake of the company, let's remove personalities from the issue. May we meet tomorrow, November 2, at 4 p.m., in the conference room?

Sincerely,

Dan Dryden

This letter addresses the issues of criticism and personal anger ("I am sorry that you thought this criticism was negative") but avoids making counter-accusations. Since the reason for the letter was a reported conversation, the writer wisely asks for a face-to-face meeting on neutral ground to present his side again and to work out personal antagonism. The question, "May we meet tomorrow?" places the burden of response on the adversary.

The original letter expressed anger; the purpose of the revision was to solve a problem. In addition to a moderating tone, the writer added information, tried to persuade his adversary that peace was in the company's best interests, and then ended with a question. The question is reasonable, and so is the tone of the letter.

MUTUAL RESPECT

Choose a tone that will be appropriate to your purpose in communicating and to your audience's needs. Audiences are usually not hostile. They become so only when you offend them by a superior attitude or by emotion instead of reason. Yet even adversaries will respect those who know their facts and who seem to be honest and sensible. Mutual respect establishes a common ground for agreement, and often those who agree can be persuaded to act.

Methods of Composition

Establishing audience and tone before you write will help guide you through the first draft. The time will come, however, when you must start writing. How you write often depends on what you have to write and where you write it. For longer projects, you will have to write in sections, and you need to keep the sections together as you progress through an outline. Longhand, typing, or word processing will enable you to pick up easily from where you have to stop writing. For shorter tasks, like letters and memos, dictation is efficient because it saves time and usually can be completed quickly. Let the type of communication and your own preference be your guide to how you write your *first* draft.

LONGHAND

Perhaps a discussion of the oldest form of writing (after engraving words on stone tablets) is unnecessary, yet few people stop to think about the best way to compose their ideas before they begin writing. Longhand is a slow process with both drawbacks and virtues. Often the mind moves faster than the hand. If you race ahead with new thoughts, you have to wait for your hand to catch up. Furthermore, longhand can be dangerous if your handwriting is bad and cannot be deciphered. If you use longhand, be sure to clarify illegible words before giving the manuscript to a typist.

On the other hand, slowness can be a virtue of writing in longhand: while the hand is finishing a thought, the mind can begin the process of revision by looking for ways to improve. Longhand is natural and comfortable, and its basic tool, the pencil, is cheap and can be carried anywhere.

WORD PROCESSING

The oldest form of mechanical "word processing" is typing. With a manual or electric typewriter, writers could (and still can) print their words. For most people, the typewriter is not a composing tool but a tool for copying. Composing directly on a typewriter saves the step of copying a longhand draft, but this acquired skill is unavailable to many because corporate style will not allow executives to have typewriters. As personal computers become standard furniture on office desks and at home, more people will compose their ideas by using a keyboard.

In oversimplified terms, a word processor is a keyboard with a memory, and it is the memory that facilitates the editing process. When you enter a word, sentence, or section and you do not like the way it looks on the screen, you can edit rapidly by using a cursor key.

One of the drawbacks of word processing, however, is the problem of retrieval. If you do not copy what you have written, you will lose important stages of composition, and although some programs make copies automatically, finding exactly what you want to retrieve may prove cumbersome. With longhand or typing, you can easily retrieve words you once crossed out. Like longhand, word processing can interrupt the flow of ideas if you spend too much time revising each word or sentence as you enter it on the electronic "page." Correcting obvious errors is easy to accomplish without losing the train of thought; but, as with any method of writing, more complete revision is best left for the second draft and beyond.

The word processor is most efficient for general revisions. Instead of using scissors and tape and then retyping a collage of pages, you can use a word processing program that will allow you to move words, sentences, paragraphs, or long sections. After moving sections or making other revisions, call up the completed revision on the screen to see if you have corrected all errors and have improved organization. Make an electronic copy of each revision so that you will not lose any important ideas. To save time and paper, it is wise not to print out the copy until you are satisfied with the revision. However, even with a printed copy, you can easily correct minor errors and reprint single pages. With word processing, you can improve without great cost; you also have the responsibility to take advantage of this effective tool by using it to revise.

Since it is only a tool, word processing cannot create or organize ideas, and even with new programs that correct spelling or simple grammatical errors, the word processor cannot make every necessary change. In fact, programs to correct errors can be dangerous if you do not learn to correct your own errors before you enter them into a computer. Personal word processing places great responsibility on a writer who must become a creator of ideas, transcriber, editor, and printer all at one time. When used to its fullest capabilities, word processing is a flexible tool, enabling a writer to have complete control over a manuscript from beginning to end.

DICTATION

Dictation is also a tool to reach the goal of clear and concise communication. Like any of the other methods of composition, dictation has advantages and disadvantages. The advantages include the speed with which short messages can be drafted and the portability of modern recording devices. The disadvantages include the dangers of dictating without preparing and the temptation to let a secretary create the final draft.

To become good at dictation, you need to have your audience in mind at all times. Those skilled at dictation speak to a secretary or into a recorder as if they were communicating face to face with their audience. This is not to say that tone and diction must be colloquial—just clear and not full of the clichés of everyday business. In many of his works about plain talk, Rudolph Flesch has suggested that you write the way you talk,[5] if you are a good conversationalist. Martin Nolan, editorial page editor of the Boston *Globe*, extends Flesch's advice in an article entitled, "Write the Way You Wish You Talked."[6] Flesch and Nolan emphasize the importance of planning before speaking or writing and of listening while communicating. When dictating, remember that you are using *talking* as a means of composing ideas. In a sense, you are writing and speaking at the same time. Therefore, since dictating is a means to an end and not an end in itself, you have to organize your thoughts before you begin speaking. Follow an outline while you are dictating, and remove the clichés, dead phrases, and ambiguities before you commit your words to paper. Dictation, like any other type of composition, is just a way of creating a first draft. If the typed copy looks good but is full of errors and vague ideas, you must then write or dictate a revision so that you can see all the words your reader will see.

For some writers, the dictated draft can come very close to the final draft. The skill is not easy to learn but when mastered can save time and enable you to think clearly as you dictate. The following procedures will help improve the written document that comes from your spoken word.

Plan.   Organize your thoughts before you begin to dictate. When responding to a letter, always review it to make sure you cover everything. If you originate the communication, either write out a brief outline or make one up in your head. People who dictate while traveling would do well to write out a list of the letters

---

[5]Flesch's many works on this topic include *The Art of Plain Talk* (New York: Harper, 1946).
[6]*Washington Journalism Review* (October 1981), p. 60.

they wish to record and the purpose they wish to accomplish. Before beginning to speak, use the following list to help you focus your thoughts.

1   Audience

2   Purpose

3   Facts needed

4   Action to be taken

Speak clearly.   With the purpose firmly in mind, speak in a conversational tone as if your respondent were sitting in front of you. Enunciate carefully and supply punctuation marks to avoid ambiguity. Some secretaries are good at making grammatical sense out of jumbled or unpunctuated lines, but secretaries do not have final responsibility for what their bosses write. The person who dictates, therefore, must spell out difficult or confusing names and give clear directions. A chief executive officer whose name is Conley will not appreciate a letter to Mr. Conneley. And there is a difference between *the company's policies* and *the companies' policies* that cannot be understood unless the context is clear or the term explained. While dictating, remember to clarify the following personal problems.

1   Spell out names or words that could confuse; specify given name (David) or nickname (Dave).

2   Add punctuation to avoid ambiguity (semicolon to divide independent clauses; periods between sentences that may sound as though they belong together).

3   Enunciate clearly, especially consonants and words that run together ("destroyed documents").

4   Correct mistakes or garbled words (dates, false starts, obvious grammatical errors).

Revision.   Dictation can be dangerous if you let the first version stand as the final version. Listen to yourself speaking, and if you hear yourself saying something that is pompous, ambiguous, or wrong, start over. After you finish dictating, review the tape or have the secretary read your words back to you so that you can add whatever further directions the transcriber will need. Most importantly, always consider the dictated version to be a first draft. When you receive a typed copy, revise carefully to improve logic and eliminate errors of fact and style. Four final steps will help you learn how to make dictation an effective way to begin the process of writing.

1   Determine overall meaning (Have you said what you wanted to say?)

2 Analyze organization (Is your sequence of information or persuasion clear? Have you left anything out or digressed?)

3 Verify logic (Have you proved your assertions?)

4 Eliminate errors (Look the final draft over very carefully for errors of omission as well as commission before you sign your name)

Exercises

1 Define a term you use in your everyday professional activities. Use the following plan:

   a If the term is general (*personnel*), write down several subcategories until you have found a specific term you can define (*personnel benefits*).

   b Make a profile of each of the following audiences:

      (1) A group of high school seniors

      (2) A peer with knowledge equal to yours

      (3) Someone who knows your topic well (a professor or company president)

   c Begin a limited computerized literature search of your term. Use a library's printed resources first and then ask a reference librarian to help you begin the search.

   d Make a topic outline of your definition, including at least two major categories and subcategories. Also include appropriate examples.

   e Write an extended definition of the term you have chosen. Begin with a simple definition:

Term		Genus	Differentia
Economies of scale	(is)	an economic concept	signifying that certain products are obtained more cheaply in large quantities.

Extend the definition to include illustrations or examples:

Extension

For example, soap costs less in the large economy size. Likewise, in major corporations, the greater the quantity of a product produced, the cheaper the production price.

2 To practice establishing tone, write brief letters on the following topics:

   a A political campaign

      (1) Appealing to Democrats to support a Republican

      (2) Appealing to Republicans to support a Democrat

b   A potentially hostile or hostile situation

    (1)   Appealing to a supervisor to reverse a decision to make you move without having consulted you

    (2)   Appealing to a colleague to refrain from making derogatory comments about you in public

3   Write a persuasive memo to solve a problem directly affecting you and your primary audience. Experiment with the headline format that names the general category and specific instance as in the following example:

I   Background: Increased competition

II   Current situation: Limited production capacity

III   Solution: Build new plant

IV   Recommendation: Authorize construction

Chapter 3

Logic, Organization, and Persuasion

Types of Logic

DEDUCTIVE LOGIC

In writing or speaking, the effective communicator must be able to justify facts, inferences, and conclusions by presenting a cohesive argument. A standard form of argument in western thought has been the syllogism, which has its roots in the concept of mathematical calculation. The syllogism begins with a major premise, followed by a supporting minor premise which leads by deduction to a conclusion that must be true if the major and minor premises are true. Thus the deductive argument:

1 Every student is required to pass an entrance examination;

2 John is a freshman;

3 Therefore, John must have passed the entrance examination.

Given the validity of the generalization (that no one has been given special treatment and allowed to enter without passing the entrance examination), this syllogism is true and valid because the major premise is a general rule of which the minor premise is a specific example. The conclusion is an application of the general rule and a specific case.

The following proposition is fallacious because of what is called the "undistributed middle":

1 Every freshman must pass an entrance examination;

2 John has passed the entrance examination;

3 Therefore, John is a freshman.

The conclusion does not follow from the two premises because the minor premise is not an application of the general rule. John passed the examination, but he could be a senior and not a freshman. For the middle term to be "distributed," the minor premise and conclusion would have to be reversed:

1 Every freshman is required to pass an entrance examination;

2 John is a freshman;

3 Therefore, John has passed the entrance examination;

Beginning with a general statement and then moving by related premises is an effective form of logic as long as the generalization is valid, the minor premise is true, and the application is based on preceding statements. The conclusion is deduced from a clearly ordered set of relationships.

INDUCTIVE LOGIC

Moving from the specific to the general also represents a logical sequence of relationships. In breaking from the scholastic rigidity of Aristotelian logic, the Renaissance scholar Francis Bacon showed how a catalog of specific premises, closely related to one another, would form a valid general conclusion. This type of reasoning, called inductive logic, is not a process of elimination but of inclusion. The process is still one of deduction, however, because the conclusion must follow from preceding premises. Valid inductive logic requires enough specific examples to warrant a general conclusion. In inductive logic, a single exception will not necessarily disprove the general validity of the conclusion.

An example of this general rule can be seen in the following inductive assertion about the economy:

For the third month, the government's twelve economic indicators show that:

1 The average work week for production workers decreased;

2 The average initial state unemployment claims increased;

3   New orders for manufactured goods decreased;

4   Vendor delivery performance slowed;

5   Net business formation increased slightly;

6   Contracts and orders of plants and equipment decreased;

7   Building permits decreased;

8   Inventories on hand and on order decreased;

9   Prices of sensitive materials decreased;

10 The 500 stock index decreased;

11 The money supply (M2) was stable;

12 Business and consumer borrowing decreased.

Therefore, the evidence demonstrates that the economy is in recession.

Even a slight increase in net business formation (no. 5) or a surprisingly stable money supply (no. 11) does not refute the generalization.

TESTING LOGIC

In inductive or deductive logic, some simple tests can help complete logic by making the writer include all steps of an argument. First is the *how-and-why* test. After every sentence, ask *how?* or *why?* In most cases, the answers will be in the sentence itself or in the next sentence. The answer to *how?* is "by" or "by means of," and the answer to *why?* is "because." Using these words will signify completeness of logic. For example, the assertion, "Some simple tests can help complete logic," needs amplification. The clause, "by making the writer include all steps of an argument," shows how the tests can be used.

In the following statement an assertion is followed by a reason: "The idea of action is especially important in persuasive communication because specific recommendations can help the reader or listener visualize how the world can change if proper action is taken." The statement, "The idea of action is especially important in persuasive writing," is incomplete. The reader needs to know *why*, and the answer begins with the sign "because," followed by an example. If you ask *why?* before the reader does, you will anticipate the question and supply the answer.

The *how much?* test is applicable to inductive logic. How much proof or how many assertions are needed to include all relevant points? A clear inductive argument should be complete but economical, and the examples should be typical. Include all relevant information even if some of the specific examples do not agree with the general conclusion. In the case of leading economic indicators, eleven out of twelve negative examples still prove that the economy is in a recession.

VARIATIONS OF LOGIC

Useful variations of deductive and inductive argument include comparison and contrast or cause and effect. An argument using a comparison is often inductive because the phenomena being compared are of the same type. An argument relying on contrast can be inductive if the specific phenomena being contrasted are still examples of the general; an argument of contrast can be deductive if the development moves from thesis to antithesis to synthesis. A cause and effect argument (if *a* then *b*) may stand alone, or it may result in a recommendation to change the cause or modify the effect.

A complex but useful variation of standard forms of logic has been developed by Stephen Toulmin. Toulmin defines logic by giving an example of its application: "Logic is concerned with the soundness of the claims we make—with the solidity of the grounds we produce to support them, the firmness of the backing we provide for them—or, to change the metaphor, with the sort of *case* we present in defense of our claims."[1] Using the analogy of jurisprudence (*case*), he develops ways of analyzing the problems of argumentation. Objectivity and credibility create the atmosphere for effective logic. Toulmin states: "Trustworthiness, reliability, these are what distinguish an 'objective' estimate of the chances of an event from a mere expression of confident belief."[2] In establishing the layout of arguments, Toulmin develops an elaborate model that can accommodate qualifiers and rebuttals. The terms he uses include data (D), warrants (W), conclusions (C), qualifiers (Q) and rebuttals (R). The basic layout of the argument corresponds to deductive argumentation (D, since W, so C), but the virtue of Toulmin's layout is that it can be expanded to include the types of evidence that will establish trustworthiness and reliability. Toulmin's model of an extended argument follows:[3]

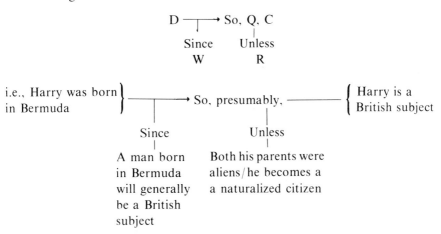

[1]Stephen Toulmin, *The Uses of Argument* (Cambridge: Cambridge University Press), 1964, p. 7.
[2]Ibid., p. 71.
[3]Ibid., pp. 101–102.

The model can extend even further to include additional qualifiers, rebuttals, and other information needed to account for all important variations. Toulmin's theories recognize the importance of classic patterns of deduction and induction. By expanding the standard models, he shows the types of evidence that can be used to *complete* an argument. Consider the following application to a business problem: We are short of production space, and since expansion will increase production, if the money is available, we ought to add to our present capacity, unless the executive committee wants to limit expenses to current levels.

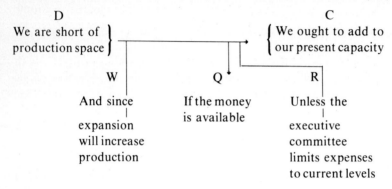

Toulmin's mode of argument is most useful not to prove what *did* happen but to influence what *should* happen.

Organization

GENERAL ORGANIZATION

Effective organization should enable the reader to see clearly your main point and the logical sequence you will use to reach your conclusion. If you take the same care in devising a scheme of organization as you do in laying out an argument, your reader and listener will find little to refute. In determining a plan of organization, select a general principle and maintain that principle throughout. An overall organization plan could be based on one of the following types:

Sequential   Describe events chronologically (the rise and fall of the Roman empire) or list processes from beginning to end (assembling a bicycle).

Categorical   Include examples that are subcategories of a main category (the business school has five departments: accounting, finance, management, marketing, and statistics).

Spatial   Describe places as opposed to events (the company has three division headquarters: western, San Francisco; central, Kansas City; eastern, Baltimore).

Causal   Compare cause and effect (cause—oil boycott; effect—gas lines and increased prices).

In each major category, only use information relevant to the topic. Often, organization breaks down when too much is covered under one category or subcategory and when the information digresses from the main topic. In shorter communications, overall organization is easy to identify by counting the number of paragraphs and noting in the margin the topic of each paragraph. If the paragraphs are complete and related to each other then organization will be successful. If a topic is overbalanced, out of place, or left out, then a simple shifting or adding of material can create order. For longer reports or articles, balancing of categories and subcategories will demonstrate proper order. Many long reports do not achieve their goal because too much is covered or because some of the categories are overbalanced. Making an outline before *and after* writing the first draft will help you test general organization.

PARAGRAPH ORGANIZATION

The paragraph remains the vital element of formal communication. Sentences cannot stand alone because they need to be explained or proved as part of a larger context. Each paragraph can stand alone if logically organized, but paragraphs are also parts of a larger context. Carefully organized paragraphs will demonstrate a logical progression of ideas.

The length of a paragraph depends on the type of communication. For example, in many tabloid newspapers, paragraphs are only one sentence long for ease of reading. However, most single-sentence paragraphs in a narrative fit together into a larger group of related ideas. In business letters, clear paragraphs usually do not need extensive data. Single-sentence "paragraphs" are acceptable if the information is an announcement or statement that can stand alone. But even in concise letters, you will need to support all statements with fact, reach a conclusion, and provide a transition to the next paragraph. If a single sentence can accomplish these tasks, do not add sentences just to avoid a single-sentence paragraph. If you need supporting data, use as many sentences as you need to *complete* an idea.

Well-organized paragraphs have a topic sentence, usually (but not always) at the beginning; supporting material (facts, analogies, examples); and a conclusion that summarizes the paragraph and provides a transition to the next topic. Between the topic sentence and the conclusion, paragraph organization may reflect the various principles of general organization: sequential, categorical, spatial, causal, etc. In some paragraphs, categories may be mixed. For example, in discussing the history of major stock exchanges, the writer may wish to begin with *where* the major exchanges are found (spatial) and *what* they are (factual). The context might call for the categories to be reversed (*what* before *where*) if, for example, the major topic is "Types of Financial Institutions." A successful paragraph develops a single idea, but each idea and each paragraph fit into a larger scheme.

The following example, altered from the original, shows how a paragraph with ideas related only by general topic can be confusing:

> The writings of ancient, medieval, and modern historians, from Herodotus to Machiavelli to Schlesinger, have been searched for insights into administration for armies, churches, and kingdoms. Studying how the Romans solved their control problems, over long distances and with inferior communication facilities, can have implications for the geographically dispersed corporation of today. The oldest approach to learning about management is through experience in other institutions. It is assumed that the practice that has been successful in one institution will be applicable in another. Certainly, historical parallels can never be drawn without risk, but hopefully general lessons can be extracted, even from organizations long ago and far away. It is also assumed that history has its uses; that the lessons of the past can offer guidelines to the present.

At first glance, this paragraph has some meaning. The topic is the use of the history, but the movement from general to specific or specific to general is not clear. The examples appear almost randomly, and the word *also* in the last sentence suggests an afterthought. Here is the original[4] paragraph:

> The oldest approach to learning about management is through experience in other institutions.[1] The writings of ancient, medieval, and modern historians, from Herodotus to Machiavelli to Schlesinger, have been [searched] for insights into administration for armies, churches, and kindoms.[2] It is assumed that the practice that has been successful in one institution will be applicable in another.[3] It is also assumed that history has its uses; that the lessons of the past can be extracted, even from organizations long ago and far away.[4] Studying how the Romans solved their control problems, over long distances and with inferior communication facilities, can have implications for the geographically dispersed corporation of today.[5]

[1]Topic.
[2]Specific example of topic.
[3]General application of topic.
[4]Extension of application.
[5]Conclusion; specific application of topic and examples to the present.

This paragraph begins with a clear topic sentence: The subject will be "Management through Experience." After announcing the topic, the writer gives a specific example. Then he provides two general applications of the uses of history, and he concludes with a specific reference to the present. The chronological sequence is clear—from the oldest example to the importance for today, and the development of ideas is equally clear—from general to specific.

Well-organized paragraphs guide the reader in a clear sequence, usually (but certainly not always) from past to present and from general to specific. You can

---

[4]Ross A. Webber, *Management*, rev. ed. (Homewood, IL: Richard D. Irwin, 1979), p. 8.

deviate from the very general rule of organization, but remember to justify to yourself and your reader *why* you have chosen your scheme of development. An easy test, especially for complex paragraphs, is to number each sentence and identify the function of the sentences within the paragraph.

TRANSITIONS

Although well-organized paragraphs should be able to stand alone, they also should be closely related to what came before and to what will come after. Therefore, the good writer will provide a clear transition so that the reader can observe the development of ideas. In many cases, the transitions are natural, especially when paragraphs are specific examples of a general topic. Occasionally, a somewhat *forced* transition will be necessary to show the reader how ideas are related.

Relating paragraphs with clear transitions can be accomplished by repeating a word (or synonym) from the last sentence of a paragraph in the first sentence of the succeeding paragraph. For example, the paragraph you are now reading begins with an idea closely linked to the preceding paragraph:

Occasionally, a somewhat forced transition will be necessary to show the reader how ideas are *related*.
       Relating paragraphs with clear *transitions* . . . .

Movement is conveyed by changing the past participle *related* to a present participle *relating*. Further, the word *transition* is repeated. Using this device can be effective, but if you begin every paragraph with a forced transition, your writing will sound mechanical. If your overall organization is sound, the paragraphs will fit naturally in the sequence you have planned. Only when the sequence is slightly disturbed should you use the device of the mechanical transition.

Persuasion

Logic and organization provide the structure for persuasion. To be persuasive, first establish credibility by including a sufficient number of facts. Then order the facts logically in a clear sequence, while at the same time drawing the reader toward a conclusion by induction, deduction, or a variation of one of the classic forms of logic. Finally, bring the audience to the point of decision and motivate them to act.

Persuasive memos follow a pattern that involves the reader:

1   Problem to be solved

2   Personal involvement

3 Criteria for solution

4 Possible solutions

5 Preferred solutions

6 Recommendation

7 Visualization of success

To be persuasive, you should provide a detailed background, including (if possible) the reader's personal stake in the solution (better profitability, cleaner air, safer environment). Then, follow with a very brief review of the general criteria for solving the problem (form a committee, complete a market survey, add staff members) and conclude with a solution that includes a recommendation for action (vote next Tuesday, send a contribution, place the order).

How much space you devote to background, solution, and recommendation depends on the audience and on your specific goal. In fund appeals, a detailed description of the problem is essential, but picturing success will show the donor the reason to support your project. In a sales proposal, specifications, costs, and delivery dates might be more persuasive than the history of the company, but even in this case if credibility can be ensured by reference to past success then be sure to include testimonials. Above all, if you make a proposal, you or the proposal must be able to answer the question, "Why should I accept your proposal?"

With accurate facts, sound logic, and clear organization, you can answer that question. Involve the audience in a problem or situation that they can picture, and then give them reasons for solving the problem. Show them several solutions, but concentrate on the solution you believe will work. Use a form of logic that will enable you to turn "an expression of confident belief"[5] into an objective estimate of the chances of success. Then conclude with a recommendation that follows from your evidence and includes an estimate of success. Short of physical arm twisting you can do no more because you will have brought the audience to the point of decision. If they cannot say no, you will be partially successful. If they say yes, you will have achieved your goal of persuasion.

Exercises

1 Examine one of your own pieces of writing (letter, memo, report, case analysis, article). After every sentence, ask *how?* or *why?* and write the answers in the margin. Where you have added important information, revise a paragraph to complete logic.

---

[5]Toulmin, op. cit., p. 7.

2   Find the flaw in the following argument and revise the argument according to the model of deductive logic and, if applicable, according to the Toulmin variation:
   a   The Zee Company manufactures chemicals;
   b   George French works for the Zee Company;
   c   Therefore, George is a chemist.

3   Lay out an inductive argument based on the following premise: The United Nations is an effective (or ineffective) organization.

4   Reorganize the following paragraph. Use new sentence transitions where necessary:

Although neither 1978 nor 1979 was a recession year, labor productivity declined absolutely in both, marking the first two-year continuous productivity fall in U.S. postwar history. The productivity of labor in the U.S. non-farm private business sector increased by 2.6 percent per annum during 1973–79. With a recession in 1980, productivity has now declined for still a third successive year. The principal development that has spurred interest in increased U.S. capital formation as a goal for the 1980s has been the economy's deteriorating productivity performance, in conjunction with its declining rate of net investment in productive plant and equipment.

The original paragraph is printed below. Write your own first before seeing what the author intended. If your revision differs from the original, can you justify the change?[6]

5   Outline persuasive proposals on the following issues:
   a   Replacing an old product with a new product
   b   Forming a political action committee
   c   Eliminating an unprofitable division

---

[6]The original paragraph, which follows, is from Benjamin M. Friedman, "Financing Capital Formation in the 1980s: Issues for Public Policy," printed in Michael L. Wachter and Susan M. Wachter, eds., *Toward a New U.S. Industrial Policy?* (Philadelphia: University of Pennsylvania Press, 1981) p. 97.

"The principal development that has spurred interest in increased U.S. capital formation as a goal for the 1980s has been the economy's deteriorating productivity performance, in conjunction with its declining rate of net investment in productive plant and equipment. The productivity of labor in the U.S. non-farm private business sector increased by 2.6 percent per annum during 1948-65, and 2.2 percent per annum during 1965-73, but only 0.6 percent per annum during 1973-79. Although neither 1978 nor 1979 was a recession year, labor productivity declined absolutely in both, marking the first two-year continuous productivity fall in U.S. postwar history. With a recession in 1980, productivity has now declined for still a third successive year."

Chapter 4

The Process of Revision

The Process

The task of writing begins with research and organization, proceeds to the first draft, and ends with revision or, for most writers, with many revisions. Revision is a continuing process in the quest for clarity. Like any useful process, revision has identifiable steps.

REREAD

Serious revision begins after the first draft is finished. Some writing teachers say that as soon as you finish writing, you should put the manuscript away in order to gain objectivity. If you put the manuscript away immediately, you will establish distance, but you might also forget what you originally intended to write. As painful as it might be, then, reread the manuscript immediately to eliminate the obvious errors that might slip by with the passing of time.

The first step in revision is to reread for overall meaning. What have you said? Write down a phrase or sentence at the end of every section describing in simple words the point you were trying to make. If you cannot reduce your purpose to the simplest terms, then the reader may have trouble understanding your ideas.

The second step is to reread for organization. A helpful device is to put a capital letter at the left-hand margin of every paragraph and roman numerals at every major division. Doing this will help you locate what is in the wrong place, what is left out, and what sections are out of balance. Often, writers will think they are organizing in a logical sequence (A, B, C, D), but marginal notation shows that the sequence is wrong (A, B, *D, C*). Identifying the sequence will help you rearrange paragraphs to put them in the right place.

The third step before putting the manuscript away is to look for obvious errors: subject-verb agreement, misplaced commas, spelling, and incorrect dates or computations. The sooner you reread a manuscript, the better chance you have of catching obvious errors. When you start revising ideas and overall organization, you may not pay close enough attention to the little details.

Once you have reread for overall organization and errors, *then* put the manuscript away. For some people, ten minutes is enough time to gain distance, but if you have the time, wait a day or more to acquire the objectivity needed to evaluate your own words.

When you return, read as if you were three people. First, be your own judge of what you have written. Second, be your main audience. What questions would the primary reader have? Is the logic clear? What conclusions would the reader draw? Finally, be a third kind of reader, one who may have only peripheral interest in what you are saying. Keeping the third reader in mind is important for business memos, which usually have primary and secondary audiences. Will the others in the secondary audience understand what is being said? If the secondary audience (third reader) might be confused, then the primary reader also might not understand everything. When you reread from these three points of view, immediately mark the manuscript for places that need a better explanation.

CHECKLIST FOR REREADING

Reread from Three Points of View	Reread for Three Reasons
1 Primary audience	**1** To establish meaning
2 Secondary audience	**2** To analyze organization
3 Yourself	**3** To locate obvious errors

CORRECT

After noting the obvious weak spots, begin the actual work of revising. In the first rereading, you will have marked the obvious errors. Now begin to correct grammar, spelling, and errors of fact (figures, dates, sequence of events). Check the citations for proper spellings *and* meanings. Add columns of figures until they come out the same way at least twice. Verify dates, sometimes from more than one source. You will not catch everything in this first thorough attempt at correction, but you should find the most conspicuous errors.

ANALYZE ORGANIZATION

While correcting the minor errors, examine the organization and structure of your ideas. Use the opening paragraph as an example, and look at it very carefully for topic sentence, supporting ideas, and a conclusion that includes a transition. The opening paragraph must be clear and interesting enough to move the reader forward without vagueness, wordy phrases, or irrelevant information. Many opening paragraphs do not state a thesis or announce a topic, and the reader is left to wonder when the purpose will be made known.

RESTRUCTURE

After rereading the first paragraph carefully, go immediately to the last paragraph. If you are arguing a point, make sure that your concluding statements follow from what went before, and do not add new or irrelevant information. Test logic to see if the facts and assertions support your conclusions.

Then begin to restructure if necessary. Experiment by taking the last sentence of a paragraph and placing it at the beginning. (You can also make the last paragraph the first one.) Some people are reluctant to do this because they do not want to be too direct or to "spill the beans," as if they were writing a mystery story. Do not be mysterious! Tell the reader concisely what you are trying to accomplish. Making the last paragraph or sentence the first often improves structure and meaning because you may have stated your purpose so succinctly at the end that it deserves to be heard first. In fact, many executives require a conclusion at the beginning of a memo or report.

Other rearrangements and transpositions will put internal organization in order. You may wish to shift paragraphs or entire sections if you decide to change, for example, from a structure of chronological events to one of contrast or cause and effect. Clear order can be achieved by cutting up a manuscript, either with scissors or a word processor. Until a manuscript is cut and pasted, literally or figuratively, it has not gone through the critical process of recombination.

REWRITE

Restructuring and rewriting are part of the same process. If you shift paragraphs, you will have to write new transitions and take out material that is no longer relevant. At some point, however, you will have to stop reorganizing and begin working on the details of your prose.

Grammar. Begin polishing by eliminating grammatical errors. All writers have their own idiosyncrasies, but some of the most common grammatical problems are:

1 *Errors of punctuation*—too many commas; misuse or lack of semicolon:

[no comma]
The chairman called the meeting to order, and began to speak.
[;]   [,]
Business is down, however it should improve with the introduction
[,]
of the new product; Safe-top.

2 *Mixture of tenses*—e.g., past and present in the same sentence:

[does]
The book provides financial tables but ~~did~~ not identify their source.

3 *Faulty parallelism*—inconsistent lists:

Recommendations include:
a create new committees;
[increase]
b ~~increased~~ budget;
[expand]   [;]
c research facilities ~~should be expanded;~~
[evaluate]
d ~~evaluating~~ results.

4 *Faulty modifiers*—dangling participles:

[the foreman saw the fabricating machine break down.]
Observing the assembly line, the ~~fabricating machine broke down.~~

Vagueness.   To eliminate vagueness and ambiguity, begin by clarifying pronoun antecedents. Pronouns create ambiguity if they refer to more than one
noun or to an entire clause or sentence. The following example contains two
ambiguous pronouns:

Local governments will not be able to raise taxes if they do not
improve the welfare of the people. This is a serious political
problem.

Does *they* refer to *governments* or to *taxes?* What is the antecedent of *this?* The
first sentence could be clarified by using the passive, and the second sentence

could be deleted altogether or improved by replacing the pronoun with a descriptive word or phrase:

Local governments will not be able to raise taxes unless the welfare of the people is improved. Raising taxes creates a serious political problem.

Vagueness and ambiguity are also caused by imprecise modifiers. Words like *rather*, *quite*, and *very* are not specific and too often are interchangeable. Perhaps there is a difference between "It is *rather* hot" and "It is *quite* hot" or even "It is *very* hot," but the degree of difference is not clear. These imprecise modifiers are best left out or used in speaking where tone of voice can convey meaning.

No one can convey accurate meaning with clichés, another form of vagueness. "At this point in time, there is really no trade-off between muddied waters and clear language, bottom-line-wise." The preceding sentence may mean something, but who wants to take the time to dive far below the muddied waters just to find dross? Clichés and jargon deaden language because words no longer have a specific meaning. In the words of the poet and critic, W. H. Auden, "When people describe their experiences in clichés, it is impossible to distinguish the experience of one from the experience of another."[1]

Wordiness.   The "clutter" of wordiness inhibits communication. Thoughts hide in repetition, redundancy, pomposity, the passive voice, compounds, noun phrases, and many other complexities. When sentence structure becomes too complex and diction too pretentious, the reader must go back to recheck meaning and syntax. The writer's goal should be to send the reader forward.

In the essay, "Politics and the English Language" (1946), George Orwell has created a useful example of wordiness. Orwell's parody is quoted often, but since his example is deliberately wordy, it provides an instructive illustration of the causes of wordiness:

Objective consideration of contemporary phenomena compels the con-clusion that success or failure in competitive activities exhibits no tendency to be commensurate with innate capacity, but that a considerable element of the unpredictable must inevitably be taken into account.[2]

When looking for wordiness, examine sentence structure first. What is the grammatical subject of Orwell's parody? (The answer is *consideration*.) What is

---

[1] *The Dyer's Hand* (New York: Random House, 1952), p. 379. This quotation also appears in Earl F. Briden, "The Jargonist as Comedian," *ABCA Bulletin* 45, March 1982, p. 39.

[2] "Politics and the English Language," in *A Collection of Essays by George Orwell* (San Diego: Harvest/HBJ, 1953), p. 163. Orwell's parody is also printed in William Strunk and E. B. White Jr., *The Elements of Style*, 3d ed. (New York: Macmillan, 1979).

the main verb? (*compels*). What is the direct object? (*conclusion*). And what is the rest of the sentence doing? The remainder includes thirty words that modify *conclusion*. As a result, the sentence is unbalanced and hard to follow.

After examining sentence structure, identify phrases and clauses. How many prepositional phrases are there? The answer is five (*of phenomena, in activities, with capacity, of unpredictable*, and *into account*). Are five too many? No rules prescribe how many of any construction should appear in a sentence, but consider the following "aphorism": "Never string too many prepositional phrases together unless you are walking through the valley of the shadow of death." Under those circumstances you need all the help you can get.

After looking at the phrases, find the verbs in the sentence. The main verb, *compels*, is strong and active. The next verb form is a weak infinitive, *to be*, and the final verb is passive, *must be taken*. By whom must these things be taken into account? The context suggests the reader, but the whole mode of the sentence is impersonal and passive from the beginning (*objective consideration:* by whom?) to the end (*must be taken into account:* by whom?). If the unstated actor is the reader, the writer must remember that all readers are not alike; their views of objectivity and the way they take things into account may differ.

A good way to test the validity of a concept is to find an opposite. What is an *objective* consideration? Since there could be a *subjective* consideration, the contrast creates some validity. But what about *contemporary phenomena?* In the context, the word *phenomena* means *modern*, but the actual meaning of *contemporary* is not limited to current events. *Phenomena* is also vague because it could mean *events* or *things*. Do you have an *innate capacity?* If so, for what? *Considerable element?* Is that a lot or a little?

Most of the words in Orwell's parody are abstract and pretentious—big words used for their own sake with little sign of meaning. These kinds of words have a name: polysyllabic Latinate diction. *Polysyllabic* means having many syllables; *Latinate* means words that are derived from Latin. About one-half of all English words come from Latin, either directly or through French. However, English is a Germanic language, enriched by the infusion of Latinate and other foreign words. The abstractions of Latin are necessary, but so are the concrete words and forms forged from Anglo-Saxon. If you desire to be evasive and pretentious, utilize polysyllabic Latinate diction. If you want to be clear, use simple words.

Orwell made his parody on a passage from the King James Bible, a work that has influenced all writers of English because of its concrete and vivid language. The following quotation from Ecclesiastes teaches by example, leading to a conclusion everyone can understand because of shared experiences:

I returned and saw under the sun, that the race is not to the swift, nor the battle to the strong, neither yet bread to the wise, not yet riches to men of understanding, not yet favor to men of skill; but time and chance happeneth to them all.

With the exception of *happeneth*, every word printed in 1611 is still current today. The main verbs are strong and active (*returned* and *saw*), the metaphorical examples are based on concrete experience (*race, battle, bread, riches, wisdom*), and the phrases balanced (*neither yet, nor yet*) so that they can be heard and understood easily. Nearly all the words have only one or two syllables, and the rhetoric reveals rather than hides meaning.

The context and purpose of writing will determine the type of language you should use . Too many metaphors may cause digression from a simple point, especially if the metaphors are inappropriate or "go overboard" and lead to clichés. Too many abstractions lead to ambiguity if the reader must define the specific meaning of the words. Leaving the job of defining terms to the reader causes you to lose control over your own words.

The Need for Revision

Patient revision will help you maintain control. For short letters or memos, revision can occur while you write if you know what to look for—wordiness, grammatical consistency, logic, and organization. Even in a short letter, memo, or report, take the time to make at least one thorough revision. Do not let the first draft be the last draft.

Experienced writers know that long manuscripts require from five to eight revisions, although not total rewrites. In the first two drafts you should present all significant ideas. In drafts three and four, you can restructure, shift ideas, delete the irrelevant, and add new information. In draft five and beyond, eliminate redundancies, condense sentences, and change words to achieve the proper tone. When minor changes will no longer improve the manuscript, the job of revision is done.

Causes of Wordiness

When revising your own work or the work of others, examine sentence structure for clarity, and then judge the value of each word. Keep in mind the following causes of wordiness.

VERBS

Verb phrases.   Verb phrases that use two or more words are *static*—motionless. Clear verbs immediately communicate a single concept. Make your verbs work. Use strong, active verbs that have the force of one sound and one meaning.

Wordy	Simple
Make a declaration	Declare
Take action	Act
Is supportive of	Supports
Place into nomination	Nominate
Send a communication	Communicate

Passive verbs.   The passive voice requires at least two words to convey meaning. The active voice requires only one word. Furthermore, if the actor is not apparent, *it must be added by the writer.* Use active verbs to describe and passive verbs to shift emphasis.

Passive	Active
My first speech will always be remembered.	I will always remember my first speech.
A new tax was passed by the government.	The government passed a new tax.
Politicians are often considered to be wordy.	Journalists often consider politicians wordy.

In the latter sentence, the passive is acceptable if the subject is *politicians* and the actor is unimportant. If the emphasis is on the actor (journalists), use the active voice.

NOUNS

Noun phrases.   Sometimes the subject of a sentence contains several words in a noun phrase. These phrases add unneccessary words.

Wordy	Simple
The fact that he was old was irrelevant.	His age was irrelevant.
A not-uncommon problem is loan default.	Unpaid loans are a common problem.

Noun strings.   Using adjectives in the position of nouns is a common problem today. Long noun strings cause ambiguity because the reader does not always know which words are nouns and which are modifiers.

Wordy	Simple
Officer analyst interaction	Interaction between officer and analyst
Word history definition repository	Dictionary

ADJECTIVES AND ADVERBS

Wordy writers use too many adjectives or adverbs to modify words that can stand alone. When revising to eliminate wordiness, circle adjectives and adverbs, then cut out redundancies.

Wordy	Simple
Completely clear	Clear
Quite important	Important
Very unique	Unique
Final decision	Decision
Eliminated altogether	Eliminated

Do not eliminate *all* adjectives and adverbs; they add color, variety, and definition.

PREPOSITIONAL PHRASES

Prepositional phrases usually modify nouns, but when they modify other prepositional phrases, wordiness results. Circle all the prepositional phrases in a sentence and eliminate the nonessential. Some prepositional phrases can be made into the possessive; others can be eliminated.

Wordy	Simple
The profits of the company increased.	The company's profits increased.
Credit was available to the organization to the fullest extent.	Full credit was available to the organization.

Strings of prepositional phrases are sometimes useful as rhetorical devices ("of the people, by the people, for the people"), but excess is poisonous. The following sentence has 40 words in it; 29 are parts of prepositional phrases.

The rapid rise *in* yen *against* U.S. dollars increased the cost *of* sales ratio *through* a reduction *of* book value *of* consolidated sales due *to* the conversion *of* local currencies *into* yen figures *in* consolidated accounting procedures.

COMPOUND NOUNS AND VERBS

The rhetorical name for redundancy is *pleonasm* (to be full or more). Compound nouns and verbs fill up a sentence with more than is needed and often confuse rather than clarify.

Wordy	Simple
I will delineate and describe the issues I believe are significant and important.	I will describe the important issues.
The job requires proven skills and expertise.	The job requires proven skills.

If there is a difference between skills and expertise, the variation is slight. If the difference is important, write one sentence about skills and one about expertise.

RELATIVE CLAUSES

Nonrestrictive clauses.   Nonrestrictive clauses are introduced by *which* and are not restricted by an antecedent. If you can add *by the way* to the clause, then use *which* because the information can stand by itself, surrounded by commas. Do not use *which* to refer to a complete idea.

Incorrect	Correct
The rumor which was false proved libelous.	The rumor, which was false, proved libelous.
A traffic jam on the expressway made him late, which I could understand.	I knew that the traffic jam on the expressway made him late.

Restrictive clauses.   Clauses introduced by *that* refer to a specific case and cannot stand alone. *That* clauses are often wordy and can be replaced by one or two words.

Wordy	Simple
Of the two rumors, the one that was false proved libelous.	Of the two rumors, the false one proved libelous.

Wordy	Simple
The economical writer eliminates adjectives that are redundant.	The economical writer eliminates redundant adjectives.

EUPHEMISM

This rhetorical device adds words and obfuscates. In Orwell's "Politics and the English Language" the euphemisms are chilling:

Thus political language has to consist largely of euphemism, question-begging and sheer cloudy vagueness. Defenceless villages are bombarded from the air, the inhabitants driven out into the countryside, the cattle machine-gunned, the huts set on fire with incendiary bullets: this is called *pacification*. Millions of peasants are robbed of their farms and sent trudging along the roads with no more than they can carry: this is called *transfer of population* or *rectification of frontiers*. People are imprisoned for years without trial, or shot in the back of the neck or sent to die of scurvy in Arctic lumber camps: this is called *elimination of unreliable elements*. Such phraseology is needed if one wants to name things without calling up mental pictures of them.[3]

Sometimes writers use euphemism so as not to appear indelicate. Certainly, tone is important in writing, but not at the expense of meaning. To avoid wordiness and ambiguity, call a pliers a pliers and not a multipurpose repair device.

The following is a list of five euphemisms and their probable meanings:

Euphemism	Meaning
Chinaware technician	Dishwasher
In a retrenchment mode	Losing money
Operative	Spy
Line the pockets	Bribe
Job action	Strike
Rolling-stock consist	Train

Pleonasm in all its forms can be cut out by the surgical knife of a sharp editor. Be your own editor and delete everything that confuses rather than clarifies.

Many other writing problems contribute to wordiness and imprecision. The glossary in the back of this book lists and explains common problems of grammar, spelling, usage, and organization.

Sample Revision

When applied to writing, *economy* means achieving clarity without diluting sense. Removing excess will help achieve clarity; so will adding important information or logical steps. Consider the following paragraph in its original and revised form.

[3]Ibid., p. 166.

By introducing
~~The introducton~~ of a new ~~employee education~~
recognizes
~~and~~ training program, ~~by~~ Morgan Systems ~~implicitly~~
the   for employees to accomplish specific
~~states a~~ need ~~exists to train employees for a very~~
tasks.
~~specific task.~~ The ~~very~~ nature of Morgan Systems'
require a
business ~~indicates a highly~~ skilled, ~~well~~ educated
professional
and ~~professionally proficient~~ work force. The ~~recognized~~
training
goal of the ~~training/career development~~ program is ~~the~~
employees to perform technical jobs while developing
~~development of research oriented individual employees~~
researchers into managers.   training
~~into well-qualified managers.~~ By ~~developing~~ new managers
internally, Morgan Systems will ~~solve the double problems~~
encourage the   of its employees
~~of encouraging internal~~ career development ~~within the~~
and improve operations.
~~company and improving task-oriented operations.~~

The revisions have eliminated some of the redundancies, but the job is not finished because organization could be improved. If the first and second sentences are transposed and new transitions added, the paragraph will develop logically from general background to specific application.

The nature of Morgan Systems' business requires a skilled, educated, and professional work force. By introducing a new training program, the company recognizes the need for employees to accomplish specific tasks. The goal of the new program is training employees to perform technical jobs while developing researchers into managers. By training new managers internally, Morgan Systems will encourage the career development of its employees and improve operations.

Perhaps this paragraph could be improved even more, but to do so would require more information than the original supplied. The original writer also might argue that meaning was lost when *improving task-oriented operations* was changed to *improve operations,* but the jargon term *task-oriented* was covered earlier by the word *technical.* Read the original and the rewrites again, and decide for yourself if the final revision was successful. Then compare this paragraph with one of your own to see how you can improve meaning through the process of revision.

Exercises

1 The following sentences contain obvious grammatical errors. Name the errors and correct them.

    a The steel beams and concrete that supports the foundation need to be inspected.

    b Having no prior experience, the assembly line procedure will be difficult to learn.

    c Productivity was limited however profits increased.

2 Reorganize the paragraph printed below. Identify the principle of organization (chronological, general to specific, specific to general, etc.).

    Part of the responsibility for this problem rested with top management. In a highly unstructured company, a strong sense of priorities and leadership has to be set by management. Yet the company appeared fragmented into the functional divisions with each person working on his own specialty. In the training area, Johnson merely acquiesced to the suggestions of Cornwall and Davis. He added little initiative or input into the design of the training program.

3 Revise the paragraph contained in exercise two. Correct errors, but concentrate on eliminating wordiness.

4 Select a sample of your own writing. Circle the subjects and main verbs and then revise the same at least twice.

PART 2
Specific Tasks of Writing

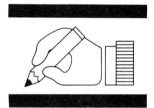

Chapter 5
Letters

*"I have made this letter longer than usual because I lack
the time to make it short."*
Blaise Pascal

Definition

Letters are communications between individuals. They can be formal or informal, depending on purpose and audience. Like any other kind of communication, letters should be well-planned.

The three main reasons for writing letters are to inform, to inquire, or to persuade. Keep the letter brief and do not include more than one central subject. Choose a tone fitting to the letter's purpose and to the primary audience.

After deciding on purpose and audience, make a brief outline in order to put into words all the facts needed to accomplish your purpose. Select a format appropriate to the audience, and then begin to write as if your reader were sitting in front of you.

Format

The format of a letter varies from company to company and from culture to culture. There are no universal rules, only conventions. The purpose of format is to create a visual structure that will divide the letter into easily understandable components.

COMPONENTS

The standard components of a letter include: (1) letterhead or address of writer, (2) address of respondent, (3) salutation, (4) body, (5) complimentary close, (6) signature, and (7) reference.

Letterhead.   Most organizations create a letterhead that communicates their image. Standard format calls for the company name and address to be at the top or *head* of the letter, on the right or left margin, in the center, or across the whole top. The date is placed beneath the letterhead. If you are writing a personal letter without an organization's letterhead, put your address above the date of the letter, usually to the right of center. Your name is not necessary here because it will appear in the signature line.

> 17 Pond St.
> Wessex, NH 03000
> October 29, 19--

Address of respondent.   The full name and address of the respondent should appear on the left margin. For long addresses, place the title next to the name.

Mr. James Black		Dr. Edward Bell, Director
Sales Manager		Research Department
Leaf Industries	or	Technical Development Division
212 Williams Drive		General Scientific
Dryden, MA 02000		Westmoreland, PA 19000

Salutation.   If you have no prior correspondence, you may not know how to address your respondent. Always use *Dr.* for people in the medical professions, but try to find out whether Ph.D.s use their professional title. Usage of the female appellation is changing. Although the *Ms.* form is not a true abbreviation, it is at least understood as referring to any female. Should a female object to this new form, she can indicate her preference when she signs her name to a letter. Perhaps the solution to this usage problem would be to call all females *Miss* to indicate sex rather than marital status, just as we call all males *Mr.* Until usage is codified, call a person what he or she wants to be called, and if you do not know what the person prefers, use *Mr.* for males and the new general form, *Ms.*, for females. However, remember that if you use *Ms.* you risk offending linguistic traditionalists, and if you use *Miss* you might offend those who do not wish to see discrimination in any form.

It is possible to address a person without referring to title or sex by using the complete name in the salutation. This usage has its roots in the Quaker tradition, but the form is not standard. Whatever form you select, double-space between the address and the salutation:

Ms. Janet Jones		Janet Jones
Vice President, Sales		————
Technical Products, Inc.	or	————
200 Ridge Ave.		————
Arlington, VA 22000		————
Dear Ms. Jones		Dear Janet Jones

If you do not have a name or title to use, try to find one by looking at an organization's literature or by using a toll-free telephone number. If you still cannot locate a name, you may revert to *Dear Sir, Dear Madam,* or *Gentlemen,* but any of these might be wrong and therefore embarrassing. The standard, *To Whom It May Concern,* is stiff, but the problem of determing the primary receiver will be left to the person who opens the letter. To avoid sexism and embarrassment, you might wish to leave off the salutation. Doing so, however, will again offend traditionalists.

Body. For indented style, indent five spaces and use double space between paragraphs. Use a comma after the salutation. For the commonly used block style, use a colon after the salutation but do not indent paragraphs. Full block style normally requires that no punctuation follow the salutation or complimentary close.

Complimentary close. Although many variations exist, four phrases are commonly used:

1 *Yours truly* (with more than one word, capitalize only the first)—often used for first letters.

2 *Yours very truly*—the addition of *very* adds a tone of sincerity or friendliness.

3 *Sincerely*—often used for continuing correspondence (variations include *very sincerely yours, yours very sincerely*).

4 *Cordially*—used in informal situations to convey a tone of friendliness or appreciation.

Each of these phrases has its variations, depending on tone and on the writer's personal preference. Most complimentary closes are adverbs (*regards* is an exception) because they are left over from a former tradition that required the personal pronoun and a verb:

I am,
Faithfully yours,

Samuel Boswell

After choosing the appropriate word or words, place a comma after the complimentary close and leave four spaces before the signature line.

Signature. The signature line should include full name *and* title. The title
records the writer's responsibility at the time. When a filed letter is reviewed, it is
often helpful to know the title of the signer, especially if that person has moved to
another job.

Sincerely,

John Johnston
Director of Operations

If you place the title on the line with the name, use a comma (McWilliam
Blodgett, President). If the title is underneath the name, the comma is optional.

Reference. The reference section includes the uppercase initials of the writer
and the lowercase initials of the secretary, separated by a virgule (/) or colon (:).
Other reference lines include enclosures (Enc.), carbon or xerox copy (cc.), or
blind copy (bc.). Reference lines are usually placed on the left margin in the
modified block style.

LMR/rc
Enc.
cc: Thomas Angel

LAYOUT

The two most popular formats of American business letters are the block style
and modified block style. In block style, all components of the letter begin at the
left margin. Some block-style letters use *open punctuation* (no punctuation
marks except in the body of the letter); others use *mixed punctuation* (a colon
after the salutation and a comma after the complimentary close). Paragraphs are
not indented.

BLOCK STYLE WITH MIXED PUNCTUATION

Letterhead

2 line spaces

May 1, 19--

6 line spaces

Mr. James Jackson
Vice President
Adamco, Inc.
117 Sterling Drive
Sandburg, OH 44000

2 line spaces

Dear Mr. Jackson:

2 line spaces

Current market projections for . . . .

2 line spaces

Sincerely,

4 line spaces

Edward Mills
Director of Marketing

2 line spaces

EM/ep

Modified block style.   A modified block style requires that the address, salutation, body, and references begin at the left margin. Date and complimentary close are lined up with each other to the right of center. Paragraphs are not indented.

MODIFIED BLOCK STYLE

Letterhead

July 1, 19--

3 or 4 line spaces
(depending on length of letter)

Mr. Robert Lewis
120 Vine St.
Chicago, IL 60000   2 line spaces

Dear Mr. Lewis: 2 line spaces

Two weeks ago, Pierce and Dodge created a new investment
program for individuals who . . . .

                                      2 line spaces

                              Yours truly,

                              4 line spaces

                              Gordon Sell
                              Market Representative

Throughout recent business history, organizations and individuals have used these and many other letter formats such as the semiblock style (colon following salutation, paragraphs indented) and the Administrative Management Society simplified style (full block, open punctuation). In selecting a format, first choose one that will not confuse the reader, and then be consistent.

Types of Letters

Because letter writers often need to accomplish many purposes, it is difficult to offer a list that includes every category. Nevertheless, here are some examples of typical letters. The list is by no means exhaustive, but it includes letters most people will be expected to write in their careers. In all types of letters, concentrate on clarity of organization and language.

LETTER OF INQUIRY

Letters of inquiry request specific information. Pertinent questions include *what*, *where*, *when*, *how*, *how much*. Other questions, of course, will correspond to the specific need for information. Whatever the questions, this type of letter *asks for* an answer.

SAMPLE LETTER OF INQUIRY

C & L Sporting Goods
143 Derby Rd.
Stanton, NY 10000
October 20, 19--

Mr. Walter Gray
Aspen Industries
7479 Birch St.
Denver, CO 80000

Dear Mr. Gray:

Your classified advertisement in the September issue of Slopes Magazine announced a new type of ski binder and welcomed dealer inquiries.[1] Please send me a description of your product [2] and a price list (Do you give a discount for cash?).[3] I would also like to know when the item will be available and approximately how fast you can fill orders.[4] Since the ski season is about to begin, will you reply as soon as possible?[5]

Yours truly,

Jack Colton
Sales Manager

JC/er

---

[1] Reason for inquiry.
[2] What?
[3] How much?
[4] When?
[5] Request for answer.

The final question (Will you reply. . . ?) might, for the sake of creating a courteous tone, be implied: "Since the ski season is about to begin, I would appreciate hearing from you as soon as possible."

INFORMATIVE LETTER

The informative letter responds to needs for information. If the informative letter answers a specific request, as, for example, to the letter above, the letter's organization will be determined by the type of information needed. If you initiate the information, organize the letter according to the questions the reader would ask and the answers you want to give. The important information you need to send will probably include *what* and *when* and might continue with *how* and *how much*.

SAMPLE INFORMATIVE LETTER

Computer Suppliers, Inc.
1211 San Ysabel Rd.
San Leandro, CA 94000

March 1, 19--

Mr. Stephen Bloom
Evans Electronics
1345 Street Road
Belmont, WA 98000

Dear Mr. Bloom:

Computer Suppliers' new price list[1] will become effective April 1, 19--.[2] Please review the enclosed list carefully, noting changes that may affect you.[3] Most prices have risen less than 5 percent.[4]

Evans Electronics has been our most valued customer in the Northwest region for the past twelve years. We look forward to our continuing association.[5]

Sincerely,

Ronald E. Lane,
President

REL/dh
Enc.

[1] What?
[2] When?
[3] How?
[4] How much?
[5] Tone of courtesy and sincerity.

PERSUASIVE LETTER

Persuasive letters motivate the reader to take action. To persuade, you need to involve the reader by giving reasons for taking action: *solve a problem, satisfy a need, change a situation.* After determining the purpose and audience of a persuasive letter, organize the content with some or all of the following components in mind:

1 What? (problem to be solved)

2 Who? (personal involvement)

3 How? (criteria for solution, possible solutions, preferred solutions, recommendation)

4 When? (need for immediacy)

5 Why? (visualization of success)

Because answering *why?* is the goal that will motivate the reader to action, the concluding visualization of success should be kept in the reader's mind at all times. If you have eliminated the reasons for *not* taking action and supplied the reasons *for* taking action, you will have anticipated objections, visualized success, and brought the reader to the point of decision.

Following are two types of persuasive letters—the problem-solving letter and the sales letter.

SAMPLE PROBLEM-SOLVING LETTER

384 Harrison St.
New Town, CA 94000
February 22, 19--

Mr. Henry Bolingbroke
Acme Taxi
1217 Dock St.
San Francisco, CA 94000

Dear Mr. Bolingbroke:

On January 20, 19--, I gashed my leg and tore a new suit in one of your taxis.[1] In our telephone conversation the next day you said you would pay for the suit.[2] On January 25, 19--, I sent you a letter explaining the problem and a bill for $159.00. As of today, your check has not arrived.[1]

I have contacted the Taxi Commission for help, but they asked me to write you again before they became involved.[3] Please send the check[3] immediately so this claim can be settled.[4] Your courteousness on the phone suggests that you are willing to solve this problem. If I receive your check within ten days of the date of this letter, I will take no further action.[5]

Sincerely,

Sherman Williams

[1]What? (problem to be solved)
[2]Who? (personal involvement)
[3]How? (possible solution, preferred solution, recommendation)
[4]When? (need for immediacy)
[5]Why? (visualization of solution or further action)

In another type of persuasive communication, the sales letter, personal involvement is equally important because the reader will have to justify the decision to buy. Therefore, in a sales letter you will have to create interest with a statement or question, appeal to the reader's needs or desires, show why the reader should accept your proposal, and demonstrate how easily the reader can buy your product. Although *overselling* by saying too much is dangerous, the visualization step can help the reader make a decision.

The following letter includes some of these steps, but organization is vague, and pretentious language deadens the reader's interest.

AN UNSUCCESSFUL SALES LETTER

Successful Computing, Inc.
P. O. Box 983
Concord, MA 02000
April 15, 19--

Hello:

At Successful Computing, we are pleased to extend to you an invitation to examine some of our new products, which may help you decide how to cope with the constant flood of new entries into the market. Enclosed is our Catalogue describing the general and specific features of our products, some of which were heretofore unavailable for people with personal computers. We hope that this Catalogue will convince you that we have the most comprehensive, current, and complete line of products available for your own use as well as your company's, and that with our products you can make a forward stride into computing now. Please read the enclosed Catalogue carefully and contact us immediately.

Thank you for your interest. We hope to be serving you soon.

Sincerely,

David William James
President and General Manager

This letter is difficult to read because the first paragraph is too long and because the purpose is not clear. Is the purpose to sell the company's products or to induce the reader to analyze the catalogue carefully? How will the reader benefit from either purpose? What specific need is being addressed? What action should be taken? If these questions cannot be answered and if the words of the letter are vague (*general and specific, comprehensive, current, and complete*), then the reader will likely take no action.

A successful sales letter should be concise and well-organized, with language that will enable the reader to picture the product's benefits.

SAMPLE SALES LETTER

Personal Computing Products
P. O. Box 984
Concord, MA 02000
April 15, 19--

Mr. Richard Peterson
27 Hampton Rd.
Roxham, MA 02---

Dear Mr. Peterson,

Do you own stock? Make a budget? Pay Taxes?[1] If you need help in keeping track of your finances, the new Crucible Computer can simplify your job.[2]

> Our personal computer is designed for the novice and the expert. You can take advantage of over 2,000 software packages or create your own programs. We are producing new programs every day to help you plan your own future.[3]
>
> How much would you expect to pay to bring the future into your own home now? If you buy before June, the new Crucible Computer will cost only $595.[4]
>
> Please look at the enclosed brochure. You'll find a complete description of the Crucible Computer and a chart that shows how well we match up with our competitors in price and performance.[5] Now, fill out the enclosed card or call our "800" number.[6] You don't need to wait to put your knowledge and ours to good use.[7]
>
> Yours truly,
>
> Dan Stone
> President

[1] What? (attention arousal, problem to be solved)
[2] Who? (personal involvement)
[3] How? (solutions)
[4] How much? (cost)
[5] How? (recommendation: read brochure and compare)
[6] When? (now)
[7] Why? (visualization)

This letter appeals to a common need (financial planning, order), shows how these needs can be met (by buying an easy-to-use computer that comes with many software packages), offers an attractive price and favorable comparison with competitors, and urges you to solve your problem with *our* help.

THE JOB INQUIRY LETTER

The job inquiry is a type of persuasive letter that, like the sales letter, convinces the reader to satisfy a need. The initial letter of inquiry will not result in an offer, but it should persuade the reader to read your enclosed résumé and then invite you for an interview.

As in any communication, be yourself *and* also be clear and direct. An effective job letter should contain three parts. In the first paragraph, state who you are, who recommended you (if anyone), and what your basic qualifications are. In the next paragraph, amplify your qualifications, especially those that are applicable to the prospective employer. In this section, refer to your résumé. In the final section, state your availability and your desire for an interview. Your last sentence might end with a statement (Please contact me . . . .) or a question (May we meet within ten days . . . ?) The strategy of saying, "I will call you to set up an interview," may appeal to some employers who want to see aggressiveness or put off others who want to initiate calls themselves. Questions will usually result in answers, but the answer can be yes or no. In ending a letter, be comfortable with yourself; after all, your past record is the most important indication of your ability to do a job.

SAMPLE JOB INQUIRY LETTER

4600 Larchwood St.
Chicago, IL 60000
March 3, 19--

Mr. Wilson Wendell
Vice President of Finance
The Kendall Group
1700 Broadway
New York, NY 10000

Dear Mr. Wendell:

Recent articles in the Wall Street Journal and other publications have reported that the Kendall Group is planning new international investments.[1] Because of my previous experience with Consolidated Commodities and intensive course work for my M.B.A. at the University of . . . , I believe I have qualifications that will be helpful as you expand your market.[2]

As my résumé shows, I have been involved in many successful projects in multinational finance.[3] At Consolidated Commodities, I created a new system for gathering information about metals trading. The firm now uses this system as a model for other departments.[4] For the M.B.A. program, I completed an advanced research project on "Electronic Information Gathering in International Commodities Trading," a topic especially important in increasing my understanding of efficient communication.[5]

I am sincerely interested in working for the Kendall Group.[6] I will be in New York during the week of March 15,[7] and if my qualifications and experience match your needs, may we arrange an interview at that time?[8]

Yours truly,

Warren Collins

[1]What? (understanding of firm and its needs)
[2]Who? (general description of candidate)
[3]Who? (reference to résumé)
[4]How? (how applicant's past experience indicates general abilities)
[5]How? (how past experience matches company's specific needs)
[6]How? (tone of sincerity indicates how applicant will interact with others)
[7]When? (availability for interview)
[8]When? (when can a meeting be arranged?)

This letter might have ended with a specific statement rather than a question ("I will call on March 10 to set up an appointment"), especially because the candidate's trip to New York is approaching. However, this statement forces the reader to make a quick decision about the interview. If the reader is to be persuaded to accept this proposal, the applicant's qualifications and experience will be more important than the strategy of the cover letter.

A Final Note on Tone

The tone of a letter, or any communication, depends on your personality, audience, and purpose. Polysyllabic words can make you sound pretentious, conveying a tone of "I'm better than you." Overuse of the personal pronoun, *I*, also creates a tone of self-importance. Use the personal pronoun for emphasis and involvement, but where you can, shift the emphasis from the *I* to *you*. You do not need to use the second-person pronoun to involve the reader, but if you tell someone about a problem and a solution, you create an *I- You* relationship: (I am telling you that) Long-range planning will help (you) reduce uncertainty. An objective, straightforward tone will reach an audience directly without interference of personality, emotion, or pretentiousness.

Exercises

1   Look in a newspaper or magazine and find a new product that interests you. Write a letter of inquiry to the company asking for more information.

2 Look on a bulletin board for a sales flyer, or check the mail for sales letters and fund appeals. Evaluate these proposals or letters for organization, clarity of diction, and the effectiveness of the appeal. Write down the reasons that are supposed to motivate you to act.

3 Write a letter of complaint. Include a brief background of the problem, emphasize the problem, and offer a solution and a specific recommendation.

4 Examine the letter of complaint you have just written and modify the tone. If the letter is too angry, tone it down. If your complaint is too apologetic, be more direct.

5 Write a job application letter to an organization that interests you. Be specific about the organization and about your qualifications.

Chapter 6

Memos

Difference between Letters and Memos

Letters can be both formal and informal, mixing personal comments with business. Letters are *external* and are used to communicate between individuals or between organizations. Memos are *internal* and are used to communicate within an organization. Because memos are official records of actions, they should remain impersonal and understandable to any knowledgeable reader at any time.

Purpose of Memos

Like letters, memos can have three purposes: to inform, persuade, or inquire. Informative memos announce actions, changes, or future events, and they are written to particular persons or, often, "for the record." Usually no action is required.

The persuasive memo is the most difficult to write because it must contain a coherent argument that will result in action. Persuasive memos attempt to solve problems or create changes. They should always end with a recommendation for action.

The memo of inquiry asks a question and should establish a deadline for an answer:

> When will the estimators be able to give us a price?
> Please send their schedule within two days.

Sometimes a phone call can replace this kind of memo, unless a document is needed to prove that you are doing your job by asking the question.

Primary and Secondary Audiences

The primary audience of a memo should be the person who has the need to know or the authority to act. This audience includes superiors, peers, subordinates, and the *file*, which is a record of official actions. Since it is difficult to imagine a specific reader of a memo written for the record, use an objective, reportorial style. Just state the facts, chronologically or in order of importance.

The secondary audience of a memo includes higher superiors, lower-level

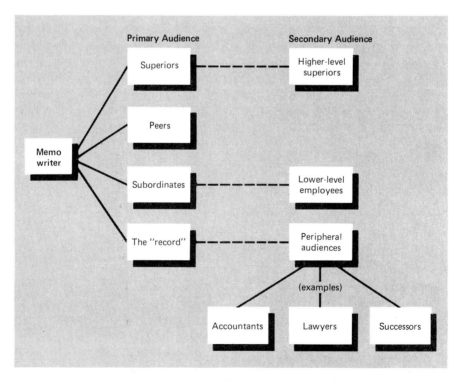

Figure 6-1   Audiences of a memo.

employees, and others who might have reason to review the memo in the present or future—for example, accountants, lawyers, your successors, etc.

Memo Format

Although many organizations have developed a standard memo style (and many have not), there are no universal rules, only conventions. Unlike letters, memos can use visual format to direct a reader's attention to the main points. Memos should be written in block form; they should be typed single-spaced without paragraph indentions. Headlines and double spacing divide sections. A memo with visual appeal will guide the reader to your conclusion.

HEADING

The heading of a memo should include names and titles of senders and receivers, subject, and date. Unless there is an established hierarchical order (chairman, president, executive vice president, etc.), alphabetize the names of all recipients. If the list of primary recipients is long, you may not need titles, especially if job responsibilities are equal. Try to be consistent in using names. To keep from lapsing into the informal, avoid a nickname (unless the recipient prefers it), and think carefully about using initials. Sometimes, using initials in order to avoid sexism can result in confusion, especially in follow-up communications when the writer is forced to address the recipient as *Mr., Ms.,* or nothing at all. These suggestions apply as well to those receiving copies of the memo. The copy list usually appears at the top of the memo near the rest of the names but may also appear at the bottom, depending on *house style.*

SAMPLE MEMO HEADINGS

TO:	Robert Williamson
	Vice President, Finance
FROM:	Raymond Jackson
	Director, Computer Services
SUBJECT:	Installation of New Computer
DATE:	March 2, 19--

The introductory lines of the heading may be in several styles. The two most common are:

Both Sections Aligned at Left		Only Left Margin Aligned	
TO:	Robert ...	TO:	Robert ...
FROM:	Raymond ...	FROM:	Raymond ...
SUBJECT:	Installation ...	SUBJECT:	Installation ...
DATE:	March ...	DATE:	March ...

Use the word *Subject* instead of *Re,* which is an abbreviation for a Latin word. Be as specific as possible in naming the subject: Installation of New Computers instead of New Computers. Some memo writers prefer to place the date line before the subject. Others place it last in order of descending importance so that words precede numerals. *Include the date and your initials; without them the memo will have no official validity.*

HEADINGS

Headings are helpful in memos because they convey purpose and meaning at a glance. Elements may include a roman numeral, a general category, and a specific notation, or the heading may offer only a specific notation.

(optional)	(optional)	(essential)
I.	PROBLEM:	DEPRESSED ECONOMY
II.	SOLUTION:	TEMPORARY JOB FREEZE
III.	RECOMMENDATION:	IMPLEMENT THREE MONTH JOB FREEZE IMMEDIATELY

Since visual format is important in memos, headings provide a guide and a summary at the same time. Clear headings will draw the reader into the memo to see if the stated topic is explained.

ENDING A MEMO

"If you have any questions, please call me." This common and perfunctory phrase appears at the end of many, many memos. If the memo is successful, the reader should have answers, not questions. A memo ending with "If you have any questions. . . ." also should include a specific reference to the subject and a phone number: "If you have any questions about the new computer, please call me as soon as possible at X5300."

A better way to end a memo is with a conclusive and self-explanatory sentence. Leave the reader with something specific—a statement, question, or request: "A meeting will be held in the conference room next Wednesday, April 1, at 9 a.m., to discuss the report." Many writers want to end a memo like a letter with a complimentary close, but letters and memos are separate types of communication. Do not mix letter format with memo format.

LENGTH AND TOPIC OF MEMOS

Busy people who want to "get to the bottom line" often say, "If it's not on one page, I won't read it." A one-page memo is effective because only the main ideas need be included; the rest can be saved for longer reports. Nevertheless, there are no rules on the length of a memo. As long as a memo contains one general subject, the number of subcategories is limited only by the number of issues needed to make the main point. If a one-page memo runs over, cut the irrelevant without feeling guilty. If your memo is important, it will be read regardless of length.

To decide on the main topic of the memo, evaluate the importance of the subject. For example, when sending a memo about new safety procedures, you may list them all because they are subcategories. However, if one particular procedure is more important than the others, you may need to write a separate memo to make sure that the procedure is clearly understood.

Sample Memos

INFORMATIVE MEMO

An informative memo usually contains two parts:

I   Background

II   Current situation

Background information may simply be a mention of the name of a project and previous action, or the background may include all details needed to make the current situation understandable. In an informative memo, avoid presenting a "laundry list"; limit the topic to one category with related subcategories of equal value.

The following memos illustrate an unsuccessful attempt and a revision. The first memo (call it a first draft) contains spelling and grammatical errors, a confusing format, and an embarrassing ambiguity from a vague pronoun reference.

UNSUCCESSFUL INFORMATIVE MEMO

TO: Howard Johnson
              Director, Operations
FROM: Roy Stevens
              Asst. Director, Finance

DATE: 27 September 19--[1]
SUBJECT: PVC Expansion
Buildings Capitalization[2]
Following the meeting at Kansas City with Messers. Adams, Wendell, and Ford, the following adjustments are made to ECE8-001, "PVC Capitalization Costs," dated 15 April 19--.[3] (Note, there is a more recent Cost Report, but I am referencing the March 9 Cost Report for consistency.)[4]

CONTROL BUILDING
10,000 is removed from the building cost code for removable floors in the computer and control room.[5] Engineering is also adjusted.[6] (The summary sheet has been revised and is attached.)

FINISHING BUILDING
This was considered a special purpose building and, therefore, costs are M&E (Material and Equipment).[7]

POLYMERIZATION—REACTION
The poly building was divided into two parts, reaction and blowdown tanks and premix area.[8] The reaction section was considered a special purpose building and, therefore, all costs are M&E. This part is 80 feet long.[9]

POLY BUILDING—PREMIX[10]
The part of the poly building is considered usable even if the PVC unit is shutdown.[11] The steel and concrete which touches the tanks and pumps have been removed and called M&E.[12] However, the support steel and concrete floors serves dual purposes; part of the building and supporting equipment pieces.[13] The IRS says that it must all be part of the building.[14] The cost on the attachment reflects the revision.[15] This part is 60 feet long.

[1] Standard military and international procedure for dates.

[2] Confusing subject line. Capitalization of "Buildings" or of "Expansion Buildings"?

[3] "Messers." is misspelled ("Messrs."). Confusing passive; who is making the adjustments?

[4] Unnecessary capitalization of "cost report." Use of "referencing" as a verb ("referring to"). Inconsistent use of date ("March 9").

[5] Dollar sign left off of "10,000." Confusion with the words "removed" and "removable."

[6] Noun left out ("Engineering costs are adjusted.")

[7] List whole form first, then abbreviation.

[8] Is a *tank* an *area,* and are there two types of tanks?

[9] This statement seems isolated at the end of the section. It could be integrated into an earlier sentence. (See the last sentence of the memo as well.)

[10] Headline inconsistent with previous headline *Polymerization.* Since *Reaction* and *Premix* are both subcategories of *Polymerization Building,* they could be indented under the general heading.

[11] Vague modifier (*the* should be *this* because the pronoun refers specifically to the headline).

[12] Agreement error ("steel and concrete which *touch*").

[13] Agreement error ("floors *serve*"); punctuation error (comma instead of semicolon— "purposes, part").

[14] Ambiguous pronoun reference (in this sentence, *it* refers to the IRS!).

[15] Imprecise verb (How can a cost "reflect" a revision?).

Although this memo has several errors and a flaw in format and organization, it is not difficult to revise.

REVISED INFORMATIVE MEMO

TO: Howard Johnson
              Director, Operations

FROM: Roy Stevens
              Assistant Director, Finance

SUBJECT: Capitalizing the Expansion of
              the PVC Buildings

DATE: 27 September 19--

              At the Kansas City meeting on 21 September
              19-- the participants agreed to make the
              following adjustments to ECE8-001, "PVC
              Capitalization Costs."

              CONTROL BUILDING
              The $10,000 charge for removable floors in
              the computer and control room was elimina-
              ted from the building cost code. Engineering
              costs have also been adjusted. (See revised
              summary sheet.)

FINISHING BUILDING
Since this was considered a special purpose
building, all costs have been classified under
Material and Equipment (M&E).

POLYMERIZATION BUILDING
A. Reaction Area
The polymerization building was divided
into two parts—the premix area and an
area containing the reaction and blowdown tanks. The reaction section (80-feet
long) was considered a special purpose
building and, therefore, is classified as
M&E.
B. Premix Area
This part of the polymerization building
is considered usable even if the PVC unit is
shut down. Costs for the steel and concrete touching the tanks and pumps have
been removed and classified as M&E. However, the support steel and concrete floors
serve dual purposes; they are part of the
building (60-feet long), and they support
equipment pieces. The IRS requires that
equipment must be considered part of the
building and charged accordingly. The
attached revision includes the changes
needed to satisfy the IRS.

PERSUASIVE MEMO

The organization of a persuasive memo differs from the informative memo because reasons for action are added. Below are two general organizing schemes
for persuasive memos:

I	Background		I	Problem
II	Current situation	or	II	Solution
III	Solution		III	Recommendation
IV	Recommendation			

The background and current situation may appear together in the first section, condensed under the "Problem" heading. In the solution section, list possible solutions to show that relevant opinions are recorded. Then, select the solution you prefer and say why you think it will work: it has worked before; nothing else has worked; similar solutions have worked in other areas.

Do not stop with the solution; move to a specific recommendation for action. The recommendation section can include costs (in time or money) and a deadline (the board should act on the recommendation by December 31 if it wishes to reduce tax liabilities). Some organizations require that the recommendation section be placed first so that the reader will not have to wait for a solution. Wherever the recommendation appears, it has to be supported by logic.

Either before or after your final recommendation, you might end with a sentence of visualization—what will happen if your solution is accepted and successful. By moving from problem to solution to recommendation to a logically supported prediction of success, you will give the reader *reasons* for making a decision.

SAMPLE PERSUASIVE MEMO

TO: Harold McGarrity
                Director of Research
FROM: Virginia Davis
                Vice President of Finance
SUBJECT: Hiring Freeze
DATE: October 1, 19--

PROBLEM: DEPRESSED ECONOMY
The economic problems facing our industry have begun to effect us.[1] Our last quarterly report showed a five percent net loss, the first negative report in the last fifteen years.[2] Our net loss was less than any of our competitors, but we still must make immediate adjustments to prevent future fiscal problems.[3]

SOLUTION: HIRING FREEZE
We need to find ways to cut costs without lowering the quality of our products.[4] I have

explored the possibility of closing one of our smaller plants, but that will result in much slower production.[5] After considerable research, I have decided to recommend at the next executive meeting a three month hiring freeze.[6] The temporary freeze will not affect any of your current projects, only the two new positions you have requested for product development.[7] All other divisions will be asked to comply with the hiring freeze, delaying their new job projects as well.[8]

RECOMMENDATION: SUPPORT HIRING FREEZE

I urge you to vote for the hiring freeze at next week's executive committee meeting.[9] Your support will help achieve unanimity within the company and will help us return to financial stability within six months.[10]

[1] General problem.
[2] Specific problem.
[3] Personal involvement.

} BACKGROUND AND CURRENT SITUATION

[4] Criteria for solution.
[5] Possible solutions.
[6] Best solution.
[7] Reason for solution.
[8] Implementation of solution.

} SOLUTION

[9] Recommendation.
[10] Visualization of success.

} RECOMMENDATION

A BAD MEMO

If you are not critical of what you write, you are likely to lapse into the bad habits that helped produce the following "bad" memo. This memo is no joke to anyone who has ever received one like it. It is full of redundancies, grammatical errors, pompous diction, and nonsense. The first paragraph has no point, and the second is vague. The format mixes the block style of the memo with the informal style of a letter, including the complimentary close. Read this memo carefully to find all the barriers to clear communication. Then examine some of your own memos, looking for poor organization, pretentious words, and vague ideas. If you can be critical of this memo, then be just as hard on your own writing.

SAMPLE "BAD" MEMO

TO: WILSON WENDELL   cc: Thomas Mix
                    CLARK L. KENT   Bucky Jones[2]
                    CHARLES RAY
                    LINDA CARTER[1]
FROM: DONALD ZIEGLER[3]
RE: PACKAGING[4]
DATE: APRIL 19TH, 19--[5]

   It has come to my attention that the effective production of
our new and important product, Pesto, will be solely determined
by actions you and your staff will attempt to make at the earliest
moment in time.[6] Pesto is a great product and the people in R & D
are to receive our highest congratulations, especially in light of
the fact that without them it would never have seen the light of
day and should be given your highest consideration in terms of
impacting the marketplace.[7]
   What we need is your ideas concerning the primary packaging of Pesto.[8] Brainstorm between yourselves first and then
get together with the rest of the group and myself to come up
with a really serendipitous concept.[9] It will then be taken up by
graphics to see if we can come up with a utilizable function and
time frame.[10] Having done this, the package will then go through
consumer testing to test the market.[11] After that it will easily be
determined what to do next.[12] Please let me know.[13]
   My best to your spouses.[14]

                                        Sincerely,

                                        Don[15]

---

[1] Since titles are not given, one can assume that addressees are of equal status.
Alphabetizing would show that a conscious decision has been made to address everyone
equally.
[2] "Bucky" is the only nickname on the list. Either that is what Mr. Jones prefers to be
called or the writer unthinkingly mixed the formal with the informal.
[3] To avoid confusion in the present and future, the writer's title should be included.
[4] Although commonly used, *Re*: is an abbreviation for the Latin *refero*. The English word
is *Subject*. The subject of the memo is too general.
[5] Standard American usage in correspondence retains cardinal numbers (April *19*, not
19th or *nineteenth*).

[6]Wordy ("it has come to my attention"), passive ("will be solely determined"), redundant ("new and important," "solely," "at the earliest moment in time").

[7]Repetitious ("light of day," "in light of the fact that,"), vague ("highest congratulations," "highest consideration"), jargon ("impacting the marketplace").

[8]Awkward ("what we need *is* your *ideas*"; could also be an agreement error, "what we need *are* your ideas); alliteration ("primary packaging of Pesto").

[9]Grammar ("brainstorm *among*," "with the rest of the group and *me*"); mixture of informal and pretentious diction ("really serendipitous").

[10]Vague pronoun antecedent ("it"), passive ("taken up by"), jargon ("utilizable function"), cliché ("time frame").

[11]Dangling modifier ("Having done this, the *package*"), redundancy ("testing to test").

[12]Passive and vague ("it will be determined," "what to do").

[13]Vague ("please let me know"—even the standard, "Please let me know if you have any questions," is vague).

[14]Irrelevant and ambiguous personal acknowledgment.

[15]Complimentary close (mixture of letter and memo format).

Memos inform, persuade, and verify. They can also waste the time of the writer and the reader. A memo is not a vehicle for self-aggrandizement but a way to maintain communication within an organization. The best memos exemplify clarity—clear language, clear organization, and clear logic.

Exercises

1   Write an informative memo about a meeting, event, or change in procedure. Make an outline of the important information you wish to include. Experiment with the subject line until you have made it clear.

2   Write a persuasive memo using the following visual format:
    I   Problem: (state problem)
    II   Solution: (state solution)
    III Recommendation: (state recommendation)
    Number each sentence of the memo to see if the sequence is clear and your reasoning valid.

3   Write a memo for the "file," recording the last meeting you attended.

4   Evaluate at least three memos written by others. Compare format, analyze organization, and test logic. What is the overall purpose of each memo, and has each accomplished that purpose? How do the memos end?

5   For each memo you have written or analyzed, write down a list of people who would comprise a secondary audience—those who might want or need to read the memo after it has been seen by the primary audience listed in the address lines.

Chapter 7

Reports

Definition

Letters and memos limit; reports expand, allowing the writer to include detailed background and analyses supported by all relevant data. The word *report* denotes a function (to convey information) as well as a format (formal report, short report, memo report, oral report, etc.). Like any form of communication, reports should not cover too much information or include material unrelated to the main topic.

Purpose

Reports have three main purposes: (1) to convey information, (2) to summarize activities, and (3) to make recommendations. Interim or status reports record activities to date without need for conclusions. These reports are helpful in gauging progress and future needs. Final reports include analysis and conclusions, summarizing all activities and making recommendations when relevant.

Audience

The primary audiences of reports may be superiors who will use the information to make a decision, peers who need to see a description of current activities or stockholders who need a financial review and summary of activities, and sub-

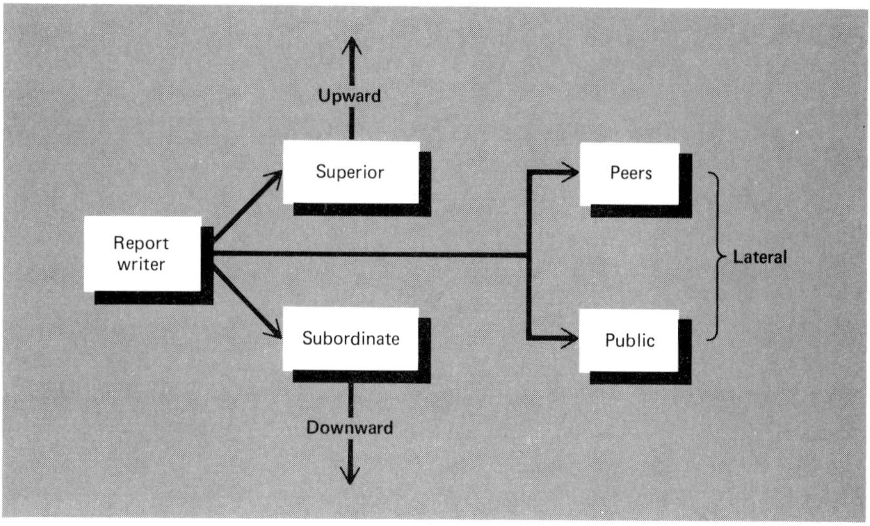

Figure 7-1   Audiences of a report.

ordinates who need to follow the recommendations approved by superiors. Before you write, determine your audience. Are you writing *upward* to superiors, *downward* to subordinates, or *laterally* to peers or to the general public? For any audience, the tone of reports should remain factual and reportorial to remove personal bias.

Format

The word *report* describes a variety of documents. An informal report can be a list of current activities, a discussion of procedures, a review of future courses of action, or any subject requiring detailed information. This type of report is informal because it has no prescribed format. A formal report must include specific elements prescribed by convention or by established guidelines.

Since many companies and government agencies publish report guidelines, it is always wise to ask for samples or style guides before writing. Audience also helps to determine format, especially when a massive amount of material must be summarized in a readable fashion. For example, an annual report combines history and financial information in a way that will attract stockholders. The content of a large pharmaceutical company's report is typical:

I   Financial Highlights

II   Letter to Stockholders

III Fifty Years of Research

IV Review of Operations

V Financial Report

Regardless of purpose or audience, all reports should include the logical sequence discussed below—prefatory parts, body, and appendixes.

PREFATORY PARTS

Documents of Transmittal. The transmittal document accompanying a report is usually separate so that the writer may send each reader a different letter if necessary. External consultants or outside agencies would submit a *letter of transmittal*, while internal "reporters" would submit a *memorandum of transmittal.* Either document should identify author, title, subject, purpose, and identifying number. A brief summary of methodology and a recommendation may be included.

SAMPLE TRANSMITTAL DOCUMENT

TO:	Samuel Gordon Vice President of Finance	Identifying Number: ECD-2018
FROM:	Anthony Bartlett Director of Purchasing	
SUBJECT:	A Review of Official Purchasing Procedures	
DATE:	May 1, 19--	

On March 1, 19--, you asked the Purchasing Department to prepare a report on standard purchasing procedures within our company. In response to your request, we are submitting our report, entitled "A Review of Official Purchasing Procedures."

To prepare this report, members of our staff reviewed all published policy statements and prepared a list of "unofficial" procedures that seem to have become standard.

> We recommend that the procedures requir-
> ing intradepartmental approvals be made
> official.

Title page.   The title page should include author, title, sponsor (company or agency), contract identification number (if applicable), copy number, and date. The title should present a brief summary of the topic: A Review of Office Automation Systems, Implementing Personnel Policy, Feasibility Study for a Zero-Based Budgeting System.

Table of Contents.   The table of contents provides an essential guide to topics and sequence. The table is itself an outline, in headline form, of the report. All prefatory material is paginated with lowercase roman numerals, and the remainder of the text is in arabic numerals. Some formal reports use a numbering system to label chapters, sections, and paragraphs.

1.0 . . . . .

2.0 . . . . .

2.1 . . . . .

2.1.1 . . . .

2.1.2 . . . .

3.0 . . . . .

Lists of illustrations and tables.   In the body of the text, tables are used for words or numbers; illustrations are used for diagrams, drawings, or photographs. In the prefatory list, all tables appear under the caption Tables; all other illustrations appear under the caption Figures.

Summary or abstract.   The distinction between a summary and an abstract is vague because an abstract is a type of summary. An abstract lists the main points as they appear and makes no attempt to comment or analyze. One author, Joseph A. Alvarez, has made a useful distinction between the two: an abstract *"explains"* and a summary *"condenses."*[1]

The following sample abstract reports the findings of a controlled psychological experiment. Although the terms are part of the special language of

---

[1] *The Elements of Technical Writing* (New York: Harcourt Brace Jovanovich), p. 110.

psychology, the meaning and intent of the article seem clear to any reader because the background, methods, and results are reported objectively.

SAMPLE ABSTRACT

The Cognitive Component in Locke's Theory of Goal Setting: Suggestive Evidence for a Causal Attribution Interpretation

Thomas I. Chacko
James C. McElroy
Iowa State University

Two laboratory experiments examined the role of causal attributions as the cognitive component in Locke's (1968) model of goal setting. Environmental incentives were found to be subject to causal interpretation but not to affect goal aspirations per se. A strong interaction between environmental incentives and causal attributions on goal aspirations was found.

Academy of Management Journal
1983, vol. 26, no. 1, 104-118

This abstract presents the facts of an experiment. A summary condenses the main points of a document and, in the case of a report, usually includes an analysis and a synopsis of the recommendations contained in the report.

SAMPLE SUMMARY

The Computer Services Co. has proposed to install a comprehensive office automation system tied to a mainframe computer. Initial costs will be $1.5 million, with installation to begin in six months. All present computing equipment will be phased out within a year. This proposal discusses one solution to the need for centralized computing services. However, it does not suggest alternate methods and equipment, nor does it address the problems of retraining personnel to operate the system. Before accepting the proposal we should:

1. Solicit a competitive estimate for a comparable system
2. Investigate other systems
3. Determine costs for retraining personnel

The summary begins with a factual background and then analyzes the proposal by noting a flaw—incomplete information. The recommendation is based on two needs: (1) the general need for a new office automation system and (2) the specific need for more information before the current proposal is accepted or rejected.

BODY OF THE REPORT

The categories included in a report depend on the subject or discipline. Informative reports describe the status of a current situation; persuasive reports describe a problem or current situation, provide data, and conclude with an analysis leading to recommendations for action.

All reports need to be complete and accurate with enough information to explain a situation or enable a reader to make a decision. Technical reports detailing research should include:

I   Theory or background

II   Method

III Results of research

IV   Conclusions

In reports where strictly controlled specific research is not required, the organization may resemble that of a memo:

I   Background

II   Current situation

III Solution (if applicable)

IV   Recommendation

Some informative reports, such as status reports, do not require a recommendation section. Quarterly or annual reports provide a sequential review of a specific time period, and although they may not include a recommendation, they may analyze the meaning of events in the time period covered and suggest future developments. As in any type of communication, format depends on purpose and on the needs of the audience.

Use of headings.   In long reports, headings act as an internal outline, showing the reader the importance of each section. Consistency of headings will guide the reader through the categories of your report.

The typeface you use depends on how your report is produced. Typewriters are limited to ALL CAPS and Caps and Lowercase. On a typewriter, underlining is a sign to a typesetter to print *italics*. For printed reports, various type sizes and faces denote categories, usually in descending order of importance. You probably will not need more than four headings.

When typing headings, use a system that clearly differentiates among categories. Consider the style recommended in *The McGraw-Hill Author's Book*[2]:

THIS IS THE NUMBER 1 HEAD
The number 1 head is flush left on a separate line. All the letters are capitalized.

This Is the Number 2 Head
The number 2 head is flush left on a separate line and underlined. The main words begin with capital letters.

This Is the Number 3 Head. The number 3 head is paragraph-indented, and the copy "runs in" (follows on the same line). Like the number 2 head, it is underlined, and the main words begin with capital letters.

This is the number 4 head. The number 4 head is like the number 3 head except that only the first letter is capitalized.

This sequence is suitable for a manuscript that will be set in type. With computer printers and interchangeable type "balls," you may be able to vary type faces and sizes yourself.

Use of tables and figures.   Illustrations are often helpful within the body of a text in order to show important data immediately. Too many illustrations will disrupt the flow of the text and, therefore, should be placed in an appendix. However, when integrated within the text, illustrations complement descriptions.

Words tell, pictures show. Reports and presentations with technical information often need visual support to incorporate complex data, show relationships or progressions, and illustrate functions. The following types of graphic information will support the words in the text.

Tables.   Tables show data related by chronology or category

Graphs.   Graphs show relationships

[2]New York: McGraw-Hill, 1968, p. 24.

Market Share of Major . . . Companies

	1975	1976	1977	1978	1979	1980
Company A	32%	35%	26%	30%	37%	40%
Company B	14%	14%	26%	22%	23%	24%
Company C	31%	20%	20%	18%	12%	13%

Figure 7-2   Sample table.

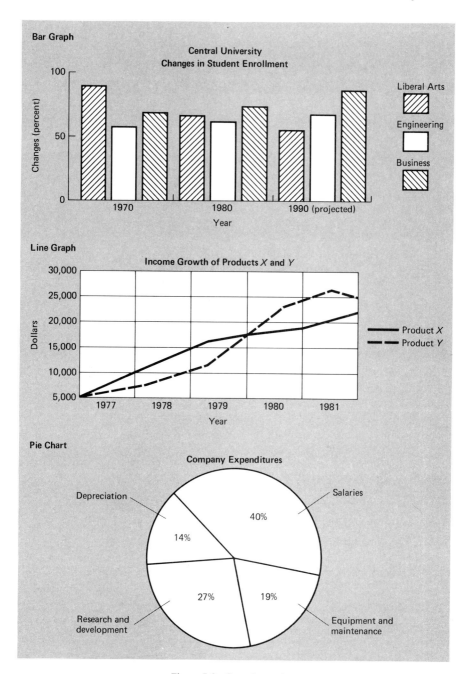

Figure 7-3   Sample graphs.

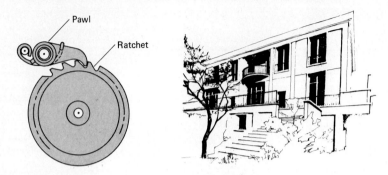

Figure 7-4   Sample illustrations.

Diagrams and drawings.   These types of illustrations depict processes or results.

Conventional format requires that tables and illustrations be labeled separately. Tables provide words and numbers. If the text contains only a few tables, number them consecutively:

Table 1   Annual Gasoline Consumption

Table 2   Annual Coal Consumption

Table 3   Annual Natural Gas Consumption

If several tables appear in several chapters or sections of a report, use the chapter number and then number the tables consecutively:

Table 6-1   Weekly Gasoline Consumption

Table 6-2   Annual Gasoline Consumption

Table 6-3   Gasoline Consumption, 1945–

. . . .

Table 7-1   Weekly Coal Consumption

Illustrations are always pictorial and are classified as *figures*. As with tables, if only a few are needed, number them consecutively throughout the text (Figure 1, etc.). If each chapter contains many illustrations, double-number them consecutively by chapter (Figure 6-1, etc.).

Place the visual material as close as possible to the text it complements. If the illustration is simple, integrate it within the appropriate paragraph. If the illustration is complex, place it after the verbal explanation, preferably on the same page or at least on an adjoining page.

APPENDIXES

An appendix contains details that support statements in the body of the report. Appendixes usually include complex data—tables, lists, financial information, supporting articles, etc. Appendixes might include:

Appendix 1   Inventory of Computer Hardware

Appendix 2   Schedule of Implementation

Appendix 3   Total Implementation Costs: Installation, Training, Maintenance

REFERENCES

The style of footnotes and bibliography depends on the style of the professional discipline in which the report is being written. Regardless of the style used, citations should be complete and consistent. The minimum information required for most bibliographical references includes author, title, volume number, date of publication, and page numbers. In many scientific publications, simple internal references are sufficient (Locke, 1968).

Do not load the text with footnotes because the reader will have to move back and forth from text to note. Internal references often save space, but too many of them will dim the reader's "mental picture" (Orwell, p. 173). If very few footnotes are needed, they can be placed at the bottom of each page but should still be numbered consecutively so that each note has a separate identifying number. If chapters have several footnotes per page, place the notes at the end of the chapter.

The bibliography should include all relevant sources, those mentioned in the text, and those necessary to show completeness of research. Be selective, however, and do not list every general reference in the field.

Write down bibliographical information completely and accurately when first consulting a source. Use cards so that you can assemble the citations according to the categories that correspond to the outline of the text. Double-check all citations for individual accuracy and consistency with other citations.

Exercises

1   Examine the annual reports of five companies to see what they emphasize (financial data) or deemphasize (bad news). Make a list of the contents of each report, and compare the number and placement of categories and the amount of space devoted to each section.

2   Choose a report topic (work in progress, work completed, new project) and write a document of transmittal. If the report is internal, write a memo; if the

report will be submitted to another organization, write a letter. Include appropriate names, dates, title, and brief summary of contents.

3   Using the topic selected for Exercise 2, make an outline of a report and then transform the outline into a table of contents. Include general categories, specific subcategories, and appropriate supplemental sections.

4   Select an article in your field and write an abstract of it, listing and explaining the major points.

5   Using the same article, write a summary that condenses the information and offers an analysis.

6   From an annual report, find financial data that shows percentages of expenditures by category. Design a pie chart to show where the money was spent. Using the same information, design a bar graph.

Chapter 8
Proposals

Definition

A proposal is a persuasive document that recommends a change, tries to solve a problem, supports a program, or sells a product or service. An internal proposal is made within an organization, and an external proposal is made from one organization or individual to another. Proposals follow the format of a report but contain analyses and recommendations in order to persuade the reader to take action.

Like reports, proposals include the standard features of background, current situation, and methodology. In addition to this information, effective proposals need to make a case for uniqueness, need, or probable success. The important steps of visualizing the future and providing costs will help convince the reader to accept the proposal.

Components

The main components of a proposal include:

I.   Background
II. Current situation
III. Solution
IV. Recommendation
V.   Costs

A variation of this outline will give the reader the additional information needed to make a decision:

I.   Problem or Statement of Need
II. Solution
    A.   What must be done to solve the problem.
    B.   How the work will be done.
    C.   Who will do the work.
III. Costs
IV. Recommendation
    A.   Begin work.
    B.   Visualize success.

In this type of persuasive proposal, the final step should be a recommendation to proceed according to a specific schedule. Without the recommendation, the reader will probably not understand the urgent need to take action. Furthermore, this step should include a statement that the proposal will solve a problem.

Types

Distinguishing among types of proposals is difficult because all proposals, whether internal or external, government or private sector, need to be persuasive. Nevertheless, two identifiable proposal types are the sales proposal and the funding proposal. Both ask an individual or organization to commit funds.

SALES PROPOSAL

Sales proposals differ as widely as the products being sold. For example, insurance companies have perfected ways of selling their products to individuals. Today, insurance proposals not only sell security, they promote the product as an investment and as a source of retirement income.

General proposal.   Since a sales proposal of any type—short, long, single item, complete system—must be persuasive, you have to bring the reader to the point of making a decision by offering reasons to accept your proposal. As in a sales letter (see Chapter 5), you have to involve the reader and show why your proposal is the best one. Include the following steps:

1   Arouse attention by establishing a general need or outlining a general problem.

2   Involve the reader by establishing specific personal interest in the problem or by demonstrating personal need.

3   Present a specific solution that will solve the problem or satisfy the need.

4 Recommend immediate action.

5 Visualize improvement if your proposal is accepted.

In shorter sales proposals, this sequence can appear in a letter. In longer proposals, the letter can accompany detailed information that would include:

1 Description of product of process

2 Schedule of performance

3 Costs

Project proposal. A project proposal is a type of sales proposal made by one company to another or by an organization or individual to a government agency. Sometimes these presentations respond to solicitation of bids or to a Request for Proposal (RFP). If the proposal is to the government, various agencies publish guidelines that demand a great quantity of information in a specific sequence. The following outline represents the table of contents of a technical proposal in response to a government request.

SAMPLE TECHNICAL PROPOSAL
TABLE OF CONTENTS

I. Summary

II. Introduction

III. Statement of Problem

IV. Proposed Approach
   A. Task 1. Orientation
   B. Task 2. Research and Analysis
   C. Task 3. Design Standards
   D. Task 4. Production

V. Program Management
   A. Organization and Staffing
   B. Personnel Requirements
   C. Résumés of Management and Other Personnel

VI. Company Background
   A. Facilities
   B. Management
   C. Summary of Prime Contract Experience

VII. Samples of Prior Work

VIII. Costs

This proposal addresses the important issues of what needs to be done, who will do it, how it will be done, and what it will cost. Placing the summary first shows your conclusions and the logic you have used to support the proposal. The section on Company Background might have appeared after Statement of Problem, but the reader benefits by seeing the problem and solution together because the solution is specific to the need and the background generalizes about the company's proven abilities. Summary of Prime Contract Experience is essential to show that the company has been successful in the past. In logical steps, this proposal

1 States problem and establishes need

2 Offers a solution

3 Shows how the solution will be accomplished

PROPOSALS FOR FUNDING

The funding proposal is a type of sales proposal because the granting agency must decide whether to commit funds to solve a problem or improve a situation. Because so many people need so much money, government agencies, foundations, and corporations have established specific guidelines for the type of project they will fund and for the format of the proposal. The proposals must show why a project is being proposed and how it will be done. Most importantly, the proposal should show why the project is unique.

Government agencies.   Guidelines vary greatly within and among federal, state, and local agencies. In simple terms, grantors need to know who is doing what and how much the project will cost. However, even in highly formal proposals there will be room for the significance of the project and a visualization of success.

On the next page is a sample table of contents required by the Public Health Service. The facts (budget, principal investigators, other support) appear in the first section; the rationale and methods appear in the second section.

Proposals to foundations, corporations, or individuals.   Proposals for funding support must make a strong case for uniqueness and merit. The projects must contribute to the greater good of society or at least to an individual or group who will contribute to the social welfare. To many who apply for grants, the process seems tedious and sometimes mysterious. Assessing the audience before beginning to write will help. Funding organizations need to see evidence of thorough planning, sensible methods, expert participants, and accurate costs.

Government agencies and some foundations have specific guidelines for funding proposals. The individual proposal, therefore, will conform to an

TABLE OF CONTENTS

Number pages consecutively at the bottom throughout the application. Do not use suffixes such as 5a, 5b. Type the name of the Principal Investigator/Program Director at the top of each printed page and each continuation page.

SECTION 1. 　　　　　　　　　　　　　　　　　　　　　　　　　　　　　　PAGE NUMBERS

Face Page, Abstract, Table of Contents 1-3
Detailed Budget for First 12 Month Budget Period 4
Budget for Entire Proposed Project Period 5
Budgets Pertaining to Consortium/Contractual Arrangements . . . . _____
Biographical Sketch-Principal Investigator/Program Director *(Not to exceed two pages)* . . . . _____
Other Biographical Sketches *(Not to exceed two pages for each)* . . . . _____
Other Support . . . . _____
Resources and Environment . . . . _____

SECTION 2. Research Plan

Introduction *(Excess pages; revised applications; supplemental applications)* . . . . _____
　A. Specific Aims *(Not to exceed one page)* . . . . _____
　B. Significance *(Not to exceed three pages)* . . . . _____
　C. Progress Report/Preliminary Studies *(Not to exceed eight pages)* . . . . _____
　D. Experimental Design and Methods . . . . _____
　E. Human Subjects . . . . _____
　F. Vertebrate Animals . . . . _____
　G. Consultants . . . . _____
　H. Consortium Arrangements . . . . _____
　I. Literature Cited . . . . _____
Checklist . . . . _____

SECTION 3. Appendix *(Six sets) (No page numbering necessary for Appendix)*

Number of publications: _____　　　Number of manuscripts: _____
Other items *(list):*

☐ Application Receipt Record, Form PHS 3830
☐ Form HHS 596 if Item 4, page 1, is checked "YES" and no exemptions are designated.

Figure 8-1　Table of contents for a government research proposal.

established format. For example, institutions like universities and cultural organizations ask for money continuously and will have devised their own format in making their case for funds. Like other proposals, the funding or *development* proposal must show uniqueness, need, and merit and must persuade the audience that success will result from mutual effort. Funding proposals make a case for support.

A typical funding proposal should include the following information:

I. Title Page

II. Summary or "Program Profile"

III. Table of Contents

IV. The Case
    A. Statement of General Problem
    B. Involvement of Organization or Individual in Solving Problem
    C. Description of Current Project
    D. Method of Completing Project
    E. Uniqueness

V. Amount of Support Needed

VI. Appendixes
    A. Description of Previous Successful Projects
    B. Biographies of Participants
    C. Detailed Schedule
    D. Detailed Budget

The purpose of this type of case statement is to support an appeal made in person. Case statements are either submitted before a meeting with a potential donor or used as a follow-up. Well-presented written material will indicate the ability of the individual or organization to complete a project successfully.

The following summary condenses a proposal onto approximately one single-spaced typed page. The summary should be included in the whole proposal but can be used as an outline for a personal meeting.

SAMPLE SUMMARY OF A FUNDING PROPOSAL

Community Theater Project for
New Plays

PROGRAM PROFILE

I. PERFORMING NEW PLAYS
Traditionally, playwrights do not have the resources to write and stage new plays without outside assistance.[1] New playwrights especially need help in realizing their ideas on stage because they lack reputation as well as resources.[2] Experienced or not, few authors can call a producer and arrange for the production of a new play.[3]

II. THE COMMUNITY THEATER PROJECT: A STAGE FOR PERFORMANCE
For the past five years, the Community Theater Project has been sponsoring two programs to encourage new playwrights.[4] The Writer's Workshop Project solicits and evaluates new plays and selects twelve plays to receive

---

readings by repertoire actors.[5] Out of the twelve plays receiving readings, three are chosen for full-scale productions.[6] Since the program began, the Community Theater Project is proud to have launched the careers of at least two authors, (_____ and _____), whose plays are currently appearing in Off-Broadway theaters.[7] More importantly, the success of the play reading and production programs has encouraged many local playwrights to submit new works.[8]

III. EXPANDING THE PROGRAM

Since the number of plays submitted each year has grown to approximately fifty, the Community Theater Project would like to expand the play reading program.[9] Currently, available staff and actors enable us to give formal readings of twenty-five plays.[10] We would like to increase that number to thirty-five and give more people a chance to compete for production.[11] We will then become the most important sponsor of new playwrights in the country.[12]

IV. COSTS

The present program costs $10,000 per year and is funded by endowment from the Barton Foundation.[13] The costs for adding ten plays to the reading program would be $3,000.[14] The money is needed for additional staff time, actors, publicity and overhead.[15]

V. PROPOSAL

The Community Theater Project proposes that the Williams Corporation provide $3,000 to support the expansion of the play reading program.[16] With this support, the Community Theater Project will be able to encourage new playwrights and enrich our culture with new ideas.[17]

---

[1] General problem (all playwrights).
[2] General problem with specific application (new playwrights).
[3] General problem, general and specific applications (few authors).
[4] Involvement of organization.
[5] Method (general).
[6] Method (specific).
[7] Success of program (facts).
[8] Success of program (generalization).

[9] Need (expansion).
[10] Current situation.
[11] Solution.
[12] Visualization.
[13] Justification (evidence of other support).
[14] Costs.
[15] Application or use of money granted.
[16] Proposal.
[17] Visualization.

Determining costs. Budgets should contain all pertinent costs so that the donor will see that the project is well-planned. In determining costs, list the important categories—people and equipment—and then fill in with as much detail as possible. Overhead costs can be listed separately or included in overall personnel costs.

This summary includes the pertinent information covered in the proposal itself and in appendixes. The background includes the general problem with specific applications, the involvement of a successful organization, the need for expansion, specific but reasonable costs, the uniqueness of the project, and a visualization of success that involves the prospective donor. If the proposal is accepted, it will be because of proven success over a period of years and a need to expand.

For new projects or new organizations, prior success does not exist. Therefore, the application should emphasize the originality of the project and the prior experience of the principles. Uniqueness is the key. All artists have their own qualities, and projects that may have been successful elsewhere may still be unique if they have not been tried locally. If the project is valid and the proposal reasonable and logical, the donor will have the necessary information to make a rational decision.

Exercises

1 Write an outline for a technical proposal. Choose a limited topic and present it in the form of a problem to be solved. Include statement of problem, background of problem, how you propose to solve it, who will solve it, and the results you expect.

2 Select a topic you believe worthy of funding and, using the resources of a library, find the names of three government agencies and five corporations or foundations that will support your project. Consider as topics:
   a Genetic research
   b New business development

c Community art museums

d A topic of your own choice

3 Write a summary or "program profile" of a funding proposal. Include the following sections:

  I   Background of organization

 II   Description of project

III   Uniqueness of project

 IV   Request for support

  V   Costs

Chapter 9

Case Analyses

Definition

Many business schools and organizational training programs use the case method for solving problems. Students receive a description that includes background and current situation. The students are then asked to identify significant problems, explore solutions, and offer recommendations. Although the outcome of a problem may be known, finding the "right" solution is not important because there may be many solutions. The function of case analysis is to teach *how* to develop answers by using facts and logic.

Analyzing a Problem

When analyzing a case, begin by making several outlines. First, outline the facts of the case. Second, describe the main characters, noting their titles, actual responsibilities, and important personality traits. Third, state the main problem and related problems. Fourth, propose solutions, emphasizing the one you think will be the best. Fifth, recommend a specific course of action. Now, put all the outlines of subcategories into a general outline:

I   Facts

II   Main characters

III   Problem or problems

IV   Solutions

V   Recommendations

This general outline will help you put into words the information you will need to write the analysis.

Role and Audience

After reviewing your initial outline, plan your approach to solving the problem. Since a case analysis is a simulation, you will have to decide on your "role" and on the audience of your analysis. You might wish to assume the role of a consultant who is asked to make an objective recommendation. As an outside consultant, you will be expected to know the facts, propose solutions based on experience in the field, and show how your recommendations can be implemented. If you act as an inside consultant or problem solver, you must still show objectivity but with a clear understanding of company tradition and policy.

In the simulation of a real problem, the primary audience of a case analysis will be someone who has authority to act. Therefore, you need to determine the possibility of implementing your solutions within the context of the case. Of course, since a case analysis is a teaching device, the instructor will be the one to decide on the validity of the analysis. As a consultant, simulated or not, your facts and logic should provide your audience with the information to make a decision.

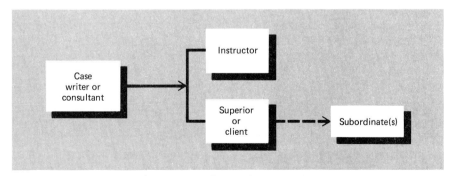

Figure 9-1   Audiences of a case analysis.

Format

The format of a case analysis will, again, vary according to purpose. If the analysis is for a class project, a double-spaced typewritten paper of three to five pages will cover the main topics. Even in a "paper" of this sort, using internal headlines will help guide the reader. If the analysis is in the form of a consulting report, consider beginning with a summary that condenses the main points and ends with a recommendation. Cover the background, but only briefly since the reader will be familiar with the problem but not the recommendation. The summary should include the following information and can be structured either with background first or recommendation first.

I	Background		I	Recommendation
II	Problem (current situation)	or	II	Background
III	Solution		III	Solution
IV	Recommendation		IV	Review of recommendation with visualization of success

In either the summary or the analysis itself, do not include too much of the background information. In fact, the background and current situation can appear in a single paragraph or section. The reader of the analysis needs to know:

1 Name and type of organization

2 Full names and titles of principals

3 Concise statement of problem

No further details are usually necessary because they appear in the case itself. The solution section can mention various ways to solve the case problem, showing that you have thought about the relevant choices. However, concentrate on what you think will be the best solution so that the reader will not be confused about your recommendations. Make the recommendation concise and include a *very brief* visualization of a problem solved.

Sample Case

Review the short case[1] printed below. As you read, make notes that will help you outline your proposed solution.

---

[1] Quoted with minor changes from Raymond L. Hilgert et al., *Cases and Policies in Human Resources Management*, 3d ed. (Boston: Houghton Mifflin, 1978), pp. 64–65. This case was written by Professor Clayton Hill and is reprinted by permission of Mrs. Luella Hill.

CARL LOHMAN, LINEMAN

The Tri-County Power Company operates in a midwestern state and serves numbers of relatively small typical country towns with populations running from 250 to 3,000. There are also two medium-sized cities in the area serviced by the company. A major part of the company's power users are small industries and farmers, the area being a prosperous farming center. It is company practice to work many of its line crews over wide areas, sometimes 25 to 35 miles away from their central headquarters. This generally requires the crews to spend one or two nights away from home, although they always return to their hometown over the weekends. For many years it has been the practice of the company to schedule this away-from-home work on a rotational basis so that each crew in a given center could assume its share of these assignments.

Carl Lohman started work as an apprentice lineman with the company some 20 years ago. He was born and raised on a farm near one of the towns served by Tri-County Power. His father was a well-to-do dairy farmer. At the time he left the farm his father was resentful that his son decided to reject farming for a "city job." Carl worked for several years with the same line crew, eventually becoming a lineman-first class, and a very good one. Eight years before joining Tri-County Power, Carl Lohman married. Ten years later his father died and Carl's mother urged him to bring his wife and two young daughters to live with her on the dairy farm. Being the only eligible heir to the farm, and sensing that it would be the logical place to which he could eventually retire, Carl made the move. Chores on the farm were being done by an old hired hand who had been with the family for many years. Carl helped as much as he could in his spare time.

All went along satisfactorily until the hired hand became ill and could no longer carry the burden of caring for the cows and dairy work. Carl Lohman then reduced the size of the dairy operation to 12 cows and he, with his wife's help, took on the full responsibility, along with his lineman's job with Tri-County Power.

On one particular evening, the foreman scheduled Carl's crew to begin work the next day in a locality about 30 miles away, remaining there for a period of three days. It was the crew's turn to accept the out-of-town assignment. Carl reported to the foreman that his wife was ill and that he could not take the work assignment because he had to be at home in the evenings and mornings to care for the cows. His foreman told him that he would either have to go along with the crew or go home. He explained that the company was not responsible for what Carl did with his own personal time, so long as he reported regularly for work and carried out his assignments. In this instance Carl's off-duty activity was interfering with a regular Tri-County duty. He suggested that Carl had better arrange to get some assistance for the farm since failure to meet his job assignments could not be tolerated.

Carl, somewhat disgruntled, turned on his heel and went back to the farm. The foreman assumed that Carl would realize that he would not be paid call-in pay or his regular pay as long as he could not report for work. But two days later Carl filed a grievance through the union requesting that he be paid for call-in pay and his regular pay for the time he remained laid off.

After the case had been heard by the proper management representatives, and all available information and data collected, the management reversed the action taken by Carl's first-line supervisor. They reasoned that Lohman had been, as far as records indicated and from information picked up, a very satisfactory employee. He had never given any previous trouble and had always been willing to do the job assigned. The supervisors in that area knew he was running the small dairy farm on his off-duty hours. They had made no criticism of the arrangement nor had they forewarned Lohman of what might happen if he could not take his turn at any time on the out-of-town assignments.

As a result of the management's decision, Carl was restored to his normal duties and paid for the days he was laid off. However, he was told, both by the company and the union, that if he planned to continue operating the farm, he should make plans to get the necessary help and that reasonable time would be granted to do this. He was given warning that if he could not maintain proper help on the farm, then the company would expect him either to perform his assigned duties or resign from Tri-County Power's employ.

Carl's first-line supervisor was not happy with this decision. He felt that unless foremen had some authority, the linemen would lose respect for them. In this case he thought he was doing the best thing for both the employee and the company and something that was perfectly reasonable. He felt that Carl's attitude had been unreasonable since his main livelihood was the compensation received from Tri-County Power.

The first paragraph of this case covers the general background: Tri-County Power is a small power company operating in a rural area with line crews operating in wide areas. The second paragraph gives a specific account of one of the principals, Carl Lohman. Paragraph three brings the situation into the present, and paragraph four isolates the problem from Lohman's point of view:

he could not leave home to go with his work crew. The second part of the paragraph presents the problem from the point of view of another principal, Lohman's supervisor. In paragraph five, the specific problem facing management evolves: Carl is disgruntled and believes he was laid off; the foreman believes he was doing his duty. Paragraph six brings in the other principal of the case—management, which reversed the foreman's action. Paragraph seven outlines the effects on Lohman, and paragraph eight presents the new problem of the disgruntled supervisor whose management decision was reversed.

The task of the case writer is to analyze the major problems of the case and then to make recommendations for *solving* the unresolved problem. Or, another way to approach the case is to show what could have been done to *prevent* the problem. An outline of the first approach would include the following:

PROBLEMS

1   Lohman did not report for work

2   Supervisor took punitive action

3   Lohman disgruntled

4   Management reverses supervisor's decision

5   Supervisor disgruntled

The immediate problem to be solved is to satisfy the supervisor while making clear the policy on line crews.

For the second approach, preventing the situation, the outline would include:

PROBLEMS

1   Disagreement between Lohman and supervisor

2   Assumption by Lohman that he was right

3   Lack of clear communication about policy

4   Isolated action by supervisor who thought he was doing his duty

5   Interference by management

The solutions needed to prevent the situation would be directly related to the perception of the problems: lack of clear communication, direct action of supervisor without checking with management, or interference by management.

With either approach, the recommendations should be based on understanding of the facts and on an analysis of the problems. If no one liked the solution, then perhaps communication was the basic problem and the recommendation should be to improve communication at all levels. If acting arbitrarily is perceived to be the central problem, then the recommendation should be to eliminate the possibility of arbitrary action.

Case analyses can take many forms. The following memo is a "consultant's report" to an executive who has the authority to solve the problem. This "executive summary" contains background, current situation, analysis of the major problem, and recommended solution. A longer analysis would provide specific examples and more elaborate reasons for the recommendation.

SAMPLE EXECUTIVE SUMMARY OF A CASE ANALYSIS

TO: John Johnson, Vice President
            Tri-County Power[1]

FROM: Evan Jorgensen, President
            Management Consulting Services[1]

SUBJECT: Policy Concerning Off-Duty Activity[2]

DATE: May 15, 19--

PROBLEM: INTERNAL ANTAGONISM CAUSED BY CARL LOHMAN'S REINSTATEMENT[3]

You have asked us to review the situation leading to lineman Carl Lohman's layoff and reinstatement.[4] When told that his off-duty activity was interfering with his work for Tri-County and that he would not be paid when he did not work, Carl filed a grievance with the union.[5] A subsequent management review reversed the first-line supervisor's decision to withold Carl's pay.[5] Carl was disgruntled because he thought he was being laid off, and the supervisor was upset that his decision was reversed.[6]

ANALYSIS: PROBLEM CAUSED BY LACK OF COMMUNICATION[3]

Carl did not believe he was doing anything wrong when the supervising foreman reprimanded him. The foreman believed that Carl was breaking the rules.[7] In this case, both parties seemed to have acted in good faith; antagonism arose because company policy was not clear.[7] The company had tolerated Carl's off-duty arrangement and had never warned him about what would happen if he could not take an out-of-town assignment.[7] To provide proper service, the foreman was forced to act in what he thought was the company's best interest.[7] Reversing the foreman's decision may have ended the grievance procedure, but it called the foreman's authority in question and did not solve the problem caused by the vague policy.[7]

SOLUTION: CLARIFY POLICY AND GIVE FOREMEN AUTHORITY TO IMPLEMENT[3]
Within the next three months, Tri-State Power should examine all policies relating to off-duty activity and review any grievance brought because of supposed infractions.[8] The company should then publish a new policy that places service first but recognizes employee loyalty, allowing for defined leeway: missing one out-of-town assignment per year.[9] After explaining the policy to all foremen, the company should ask the foremen to communicate the policy to linemen.[9]

RECOMMENDATION: IMPLEMENT POLICY BY JULY 15, 19--[3]
Tri-State's policy committee should establish clear procedures concerning activities that might interfere with the company's responsibilities to its customers and stockholders.[10] This policy should be published by July 15, 19-- and explained personally to all linemen by their foremen.[10] By creating and communicating this policy, the company will clarify the rules and restore the confidence and authority of the foremen and the morale of the linemen.[11]

---

[1] Titles of sender and receiver.
[2] Descriptive subject of memo.
[3] Descriptive headings.
[4] Cause of problem.

[5] Actions of individuals involved.
[6] Summary of problem.
[7] Analysis of problem.
[8] Solution.
[9] Extension of solution.
[10] Specific recommendation.
[11] Predicted result of recommendation.

This memo emphasized the recommendation, making specific the solution in the previous section. As in any "case," especially a hypothetical situation, "right" or "wrong" answers are a matter of judgment. What may be right for the company may be wrong for an individual employee. Nevertheless, with the proper use of fact and logic, the solution at least will have validity, and if the solution is valid in a hypothetical situation, a similar solution might work for a real problem.

Exercises

1   Select several articles from the business page of the local newspaper or from the *Wall Street Journal*. Identify articles that describe a problem and write an outline for a case analysis. Include facts, principal characters, main problem, solution, and recommendation. Since solutions depend on audience, be sure to define the major "stakeholders," and find a solution that either would satisfy one group of stakeholders or would be generally acceptable to all participants.

2   Printed below is a simulated problem faced by a company that has just been acquired by another, slightly larger, firm. Write a one-page analysis of this case, using the basic outline of problem, solution, and recommendation.

AMERICAN CONTROL DEVICES, INC.

Newspaper Item: "After three months of official negotiation, Consolidated Engineering and American Control Devices announced that they would merge on July 1. Executives of Consolidated assured all employees of American Control that they would do their best to keep everybody working."

On July 8, William Jennings, president of Consolidated Engineering, and Ted Sanford, former president of American Control Devices, issued the following memorandum:

TO: All Division Heads of American Control
                   Devices

FROM: William Jennings, President
                   Consolidated Engineering
                   Ted Sanford, Vice President
                   Consolidated Engineering

SUBJECT: Census of Employees

DATE: July 8, 19--

We would appreciate your sending an accurate list of all your department personnel and their duties so we can facilitate the merger of our two companies. Our goal is to provide stockholders with the best return on investment, and we intend to do this by improving productivity. To accomplish this goal, it may be necessary to reassign certain personnel, especially where duplications exist with current Consolidated Engineering activities.

After receiving and verifying your lists, we will make appropriate changes and return a new employee list to all departments. Thank you for your cooperation.

When the division heads received this memo, they immediately feared that everyone's job was in danger. Since nearly all the division heads had worked for American Control Devices for more than ten years, they decided to respond as a group to what they believed was a threatening memo. The group selected their most senior member to reply. He wrote the following response, checked it with his colleagues, and sent it to the new president.

TO: William Jennings
                   President, Consolidated Engineering

FROM: Bill Murphy
                   Head, Research and Development
                   American Control Devices

SUBJECT: Employee Census

DATE: July 10, 19--

My colleagues and I have decided that we
wish to comply with your request for an
employee census. However, before we send
the required list, we would like to meet with
you to discuss why you want the list and what
you plan to do with it. As loyal employees of
the American Control Devices division, we
believe we will have valuable suggestions on
the apparent restructuring of our company.

When President Jennings received this memo, he called in Vice
President Sanford and said: "We've got a problem, Ted. I want you to
solve it."

Chapter 10
Résumés

Definition

A résumé is an autobiography whose purpose is to show a perspective employer who you are and what you can do. It should be honest, objective, and uninflated. Most of all, it should reflect your own personality. While there are many styles, you need to create a résumé that will emphasize your unique attributes. A résumé will not by itself result in a job, but it can convince an employer to interview you. Furthermore, it represents you to decision makers before, during, and after an interview.

Types

The French word résumé, meaning *summary*, has been assimilated into the English language. Other similar terms include data sheet, CV (*Curriculum Vitae*, or particulars of one's life), and dossier. A dossier has all the information contained in a résumé but adds college transcripts, letters of recommendation, and other supporting documents. Because a résumé is a summary, it is usually restricted to one page; a *Curriculum Vitae* is contained on as many pages as necessary.

Résumés show a reader what you have done and when you accomplished major tasks. If you choose to emphasize the *when* of your life, you will write a chronological résumé, listing in reverse order relevant information from high school or college to the present. People with relatively little work experience usually prepare a chronological résumé. If you have worked for many years in a variety of important jobs, you should consider writing a functional résumé, in which you emphasize skills and experience. Many times you perform the same tasks for more than one organization. When that happens, what you do is more important than when you have done it.

Content

All résumés must include name and address, education, and experience. Other sections are optional but helpful. When starting to write a résumé, consider the following outlines.

Chronological	Functional
I. Name and address	I. Name and address
II. Objective	II. Objective
III. Qualifications (optional)	III. Qualifications by category (essential)
IV. Education	IV. Education
V. Experience	V. Special achievements
VI. Special achievements	VI. Personal data
VII. Personal data	

NAME AND ADDRESS

To make the name on your résumé consistent with everything else you send, use the name you put on checks or letters. If your résumé has your full name (Daniel Bruce Williams) and your correspondence has a shortened name (Dan Williams), an employer with many applicants may make two separate files for you.

If you have a common name, use a middle initial to distinguish you from soundalikes. Give a complete current address and phone number. If you have a temporary and a permanent address, include both. If prudent, list a work address. If a prospective employer cannot contact you, you will not get the job.

OBJECTIVE

This section is optional. Many "objectives" are either vague and meaningless or too specific and limiting. The objective section can be helpful, however, because here you will tell the readers what you want to do, and the readers can immediately see if they have the type of job you want. For this reason, some personnel managers believe a résumé is incomplete without an objective section, but others discount it and try to decide for themselves if education and experience warrant an interview. If you decide to use an objective section, avoid hyperbole. A few sample objectives follow.

Meaningless objective.   "A position in finance with emphasis on portfolio management and administration of domestic or multinational accounts." That means you want to work for a financial firm, but you will do just about anything for anybody, here or abroad.

Aggressive objective.   "A challenging position in top management utilizing my proven abilities to do executive caliber work." Words like challenging are unnecessary. Would you say you wanted a job that was not challenging? Avoid telling people how good you are by using clichés like "executive caliber." Let your qualifications speak for themselves.

Limiting objective.   "A position in the field of consumer electronics, including the development of high-fidelity audio equipment." Most people writing their first résumé cannot afford to be so specific. However, if you want a specific type of job, a limiting objective will save you and the interviewer time. A limiting objective may also be useful if you want to change fields. For example, your résumé might show extensive experience in one area, but you want to start a new career. A nurse who was head of an intensive care unit may go back to school for a business degree. The résumé will show administrative capability as unit head but need not mention a specific field: "A position in *personnel administration* requiring *proven* leadership ability and interpersonal communication skills." Emphasizing the type of job (*personnel administration*) and experience (*proven ability*) will demonstrate qualifications, experience, ability, and direction.

QUALIFICATIONS

Instead of beginning with an "objective," some people prefer to summarize their qualifications after their name and address. A qualification section is a general summary of work experience by function. List qualifications if they are unique or significant.

Sample qualifications.   "Ability to coordinate major projects (budget over $5 million), manage large departments, and participate in strategic planning. Skilled in interpersonal relations, communication, and motivation." Such qualifications demand support from the résumé itself. For people with major achievements in their background, a list of qualifications based on experience will immediately attract a reader's interest.

EDUCATION

People who have spent many years at important jobs should begin with work experience. Those with little experience or with degrees from well-known schools should list education first in order to emphasize potential.

In the education section and throughout the résumé, use reverse chronological order. Include name and address of school, degree granted, and date of attendance:

> University of California, Berkeley
> M.S., Engineering, 1977-79

If the information is relevant, summarize courses taken and give titles of theses, dissertations, significant projects, and academic honors. Include extracurricular activities only if they are relevant—club officer, student government, entrepreneurial ventures. In the education section, include high school only if you distinguished yourself there. Being president of the student government or editor of the newspaper or yearbook clearly demonstrates early managerial potential and communication skills.

EXPERIENCE

The section on experience shows what you have done and implies what you can do. List all full-time jobs (a gap raises suspicions) in reverse chronological order. Include name of organization, address, your title, and dates of employment. Then give details, noting special achievements such as successful projects, number of people managed, size of budget. Numbers quantify your capabilities and enable an employer to compare what you have done with what the organization needs to accomplish. List part-time or summer jobs only if work experience was significant: summer internship, acting manager, scientific research.

In describing job responsibilities, use strong active verbs that emphasize ability:

> <u>Negotiated</u> settlement with local government.
> <u>Designed</u> and implemented tax reimbursement policy.
> <u>Created</u> new division.
> <u>Saved</u> over $700,000 by consolidating trust accounts.

In describing any job, do not evaluate your own performance or give too many details. Use the description to raise the reader's interest. Further explanation will be welcome in a personal interview.

SPECIAL ACHIEVEMENTS

If you have received a fellowship, grant, or award, or if you have done something noteworthy, your achievement should be emphasized in the résumé. For example, if you developed an enzyme used in textiles, do not list your research under "College Textile Club." And if you won an international bicycle race, do not hide the accomplishment under "extracurricular sports." Give these achievements the emphasis that will make an interviewer want to ask about something you have done well.

PERSONAL DATA

This section should show your *human* side with information that might inspire questions from an interviewer. Include hobbies or activities that do not fit into the "special achievement" section, but do not try to make yourself sound mundane: "Enjoy cooking, jogging, movies." Either say nothing or name unusual hobbies: spelunking, ballet instructor, building musical instruments.

Languages are especially important for intercultural communication. Since knowing a language demonstrates discipline and understanding of another culture, list all language skills: "Fluent in French; reading knowledge of German and Italian."

According to fair employment practice laws, it is illegal to ask a candidate about marital status, religion, place of birth, age, disability, and many other questions that would place an undue burden on a person. Most people leave this information out of the résumé, but occasionally some want it known that their spouses will come with them and might need to find a job. Others believe that being married suggests stability. Since the résumé is about you, and not someone else, ask about employment for a spouse after you are offered the job.

Noting the state of your health is usually unnecessary. If your health is bad, you do not need to point that out unless you want to prevent discrimination or alert an employer that a health problem will not affect job performance. Since it is illegal for employers to ask about health, you need only bring out information that you think is relevant.

It is also illegal to require a picture on or with a résumé. Some candidates like to include one so that they can be remembered, and some personnel managers like to see a picture so that they can distinguish among the many résumés they receive weekly. A picture will not do you much good if your qualifications are lacking, and if your qualifications are good the picture is irrelevant.

If you use a personal data section, be sure to include some interesting information that shows broad interests and qualifications outside your work experience. Good interviewers will try to ask you about everything on your résumé. They might use the personal data section just to have you talk about something important to you, or they might have similar interests. You can use personal data to help you if the information is enlightening.

REFERENCES

List the names of references only if they are important people who know you well. Save space by eliminating the obvious: "References available upon request." If asked during an interview, you can supply names or include them on a job application form.

Format

There is no standard format for résumés. The reader needs to see clearly delineated sections, adequate spacing, and readable typing or printing. The résumé writer needs to be consistent in the use of headings and parallel structure and in the approximate value given to each entry.

SPACING, MARGINS, AND HEADINGS

Use margins that are at least one inch on the left and one half inch on the right. Be especially careful not to make the résumé look unplanned by going too near the right edge. Headings of major categories may be placed on the left margin or in the center.

Left margin.   This format leaves white space on the left, providing a clean visual effect. However, the amount of space needed reduces the amount of space available for the important facts in each entry.

NAME AND	Charles Wilson
ADDRESS	113 Yorba Linda Dr.
	San Francisco, CA 94000
	(415) 555-1212
OBJECTIVE	An entry-level position in space technology requiring . . .
EDUCATION	University of . . .
EXPERIENCE	Rockwell International . . .
	Project Engineer . . .
PERSONAL INFORMATION	Born, San Francisco, 19-- [this information optional]; fluent in Spanish and Korean; . . .

Centered.   Centering headlines will leave more space for important information, especially helpful if you want to limit the résumé to one page.

```
                    Charles Wilson
                  113 Yorba Linda Dr.
                 San Francisco, CA 94000
                    (415) 555-1212




                        OBJECTIVE
       An entry-level position in space technology requiring . . .


                        EDUCATION
       University of California (Irvine), B.S., Physics, 19--


                        EXPERIENCE
       Rockwell International, Los Angeles, CA          1978-1982
         Project Engineer .......................................


                    PERSONAL INFORMATION
       Born, San Francisco .......................................
```

Spacing of résumés can be adjusted according to the amount of material needed per page. Spacing differentiates sections. Conventional résumés provide double space between major categories and entries and single space within each entry. (See sample at the end of this chapter.) Be consistent in providing this necessary convenience for the reader.

GRAMMAR AND PUNCTUATION

Grammatical form.   Should you use present or past tense, personal pronouns, periods? To answer these questions, write one section carefully and repeat the format in subsequent sections. Leave out the first person pronoun (*I*) because you will have to repeat it and because the reader understands who has completed the action you describe. Begin descriptions with strong, active verbs in the *past tense for completed activities* and *present tense for current activities*. A list of words to remember includes:

created	produced
directed	budgeted
managed	administered
completed	negotiated
wrote	presented

and any others that describe specific accomplishments.

For longer descriptions, write in complete sentences, using articles but eliminating the first-person pronoun:

> Negotiated standard purchasing agreements for five of the Acme Corporation's 20 divisions. These agreements saved the company $200,000.

Parellelism. Consistency is difficult to achieve but necessary in order to demonstrate clarity of thought and organization. Check all headings, subheadings, and descriptions to see if they correspond in form. For example, list place, activities, and dates in the same way regardless of section, and use the same horizontal spacing:

EDUCATION
University of Wisconsin (Madison), B.A., History   1975-1979
    Concentration in Modern European History with related . . .

EXPERIENCE
General Electric Co. (Schenectady, NY)   1979 to present
    Project Engineer . . . .

Punctuation. Since résumés are outlines, end punctuation is unnecessary for short entries. To be consistent, then, you do not need a period at the end of a longer description. However, to some people, eliminating the period at the end of a complete sentence looks (and is) wrong, according to the rules of sentence punctuation. Decide for yourself which "rules" to follow or mix rules as follows: no period after short sentences; period at the end of a complete sentence.

Length. The length of a résumé is dictated by the amount of information needed to give a complete characterization. One-page résumés are useful because they give a concise summary of activities. If you need a longer résumé, divide it into two parts. In the first, summarize education and experience; in the second, include details such as publications, longer descriptions of important projects, memberships in professional organizations, committees, and community involvement.

Production

TYPED OR PRINTED?

Should you type a résumé or have it printed? Let your personality and your audience dictate. A clearly printed résumé is reasonably inexpensive and impressive to corporate interviewers. A clearly typed résumé is appropriate for academic institutions and small organizations that are sometimes offended by the mass production of a printed résumé. White paper is common and acceptable, but a light color like beige or ivory might cause your résumé to stand out among the others. Make your résumé look interesting but not like an advertising flyer; good interviewers care more about content than format. Since they also demand a current résumé, be prepared to revise as often as every three or four months or whenever something significant needs to be added.

PROOFREADING

Before sending a résumé, proofread it carefully. You do not want to prove that you make careless mistakes. Look especially for spelling errors or lapses in chronology. Check margins and spacing for consistency and search for wordiness or hyperbole. Exchange places with your reader, and as you examine your own résumé, ask yourself the questions an interviewer might ask.

Sample Résumés

Following are samples of two styles of résumés—chronological and functional. Functional résumés are useful to people who have had a long career of significant experience.

SAMPLE CHRONOLOGICAL RÉSUMÉ

Charles L. Collins

Home Address
111 Anderson Avenue
Philadelphia, PA 19000
(215) 555-1212

Work Address
Pennsylvania National Bank
Philadelphia, PA 19000
(215) 555-1000, x307

EDUCATION

THE WHARTON SCHOOL, UNIVERSITY OF
    PENNSYLVANIA   1981-1982

M.B.A., Finance, 1982

Major in Finance integrating Business Planning, Financial
Reporting, Banking, and International Accounting.

Complementary courses include Marketing and Organizational Behavior

UNIVERSITY OF PENNSYLVANIA,
    PHILADELPHIA, PA   1975-1978

B.S., Economics, 1978

Major in Economics with concentration in International
Finance; minor in English. Awarded Ronald Jones Prize for
best senior thesis in Economics: "The Effect of the World
Bank on Developing Countries."

EXPERIENCE

THE PENNSYLVANIA NATIONAL BANK,
    PHILADELPHIA, PA   1982--

Latin American Relations Manager

Managed the bank's relationships with a group of Central and
South American Corporations. Developed and implemented
account strategies. Administered existing lending agreements.

Credit Analyst

Participated in Credit Training Program emphasizing preparation of financial statements, cash flow analysis and market
studies. Prepared credit reports and marketing recommendations.

CORPORATE CONSULTANTS, INC.,
    NEW YORK, NY   1978-1981

Foreign Trade Advisor

Created Foreign trade department of major consulting firm.
Analyzed, estimated, and projected Brazilian trade balance
with emphasis on Latin American trade agreements.

PERSONAL DATA

U.S. citizen, born in Brazil. Fluent in English, Portuguese, and
Italian. Played competitive tennis. Advanced photographer.

SAMPLE FUNCTIONAL RÉSUMÉ

NAME AND ADDRESS	Thomas E. Elliott 918 Vine Street Kansas City, MO 64000 (816) 555-1212
OBJECTIVE	A position in fund raising with a large public institution

EXPERIENCE AND ACHIEVEMENTS	Developing funding strategies
	    Identifying corporations, foundations and individuals for active participation in major educational and cultural projects
	Improving planning and financing
	    Initiating plans for major capital campaigns in excess of $255 million
	Increasing public relations effectiveness
	Creating proposals for major capital improvements and new programs

EMPLOYERS	Clinton Museum of Art, 1980-Present
	  Boston, MA
	  Director of Development
	
	Mid-Atlantic College, 1975-1980
	  Allen, PA
	  Development Officer

EDUCATION	Tufts University, 1971-1975
	  Medford, MA
	  B.A., Art History

FINAL REVIEW

Before sending your résumé, look it over one more time. Are there any errors? If so, correct them in pen rather than send something that is wrong. Have you emphasized your experience and achievements well enough to distinguish you from other candidates? What questions does your résumé answer? What questions will an interviewer ask after reading your résumé? The résumé represents you before, during, and after an interview. If your résumé is accurate and convincing, you will be well-represented.

Exercises

1   Make a list of important facts about you, beginning with high school. Include degrees, awards, special achievements, community service, and any other unique information.

2   List all work experiences including summer, full- and part-time jobs, paid and volunteer. Include organization and duties.

3   Analyze work and educational experience, and make a list of the functions you have performed (administered budgets, managed people, initiated new projects, etc.).

4   Choose a company you would like to work for and write a job objective specifically suited to that company's needs and to your qualifications. Write another job objective that emphasizes your general objective regardless of company.

5   Write a "qualifications" section, showing the skills you have acquired as a result of your education and work experience.

6   Write a chronological résumé, and then write a functional résumé using the same information. Experiment with format.

PART 3

General Principles of Speaking

Chapter 11
Organization

Organizing a speech and organizing a written document should not differ very much because both inform, persuade, or inquire. (See Chapter 3.) The organization of a speech must be simple enough to lead an audience *forward* through a logical progression of ideas. Readers can go backward to reconsider complexities; listeners can only go in the direction the speaker takes them.

A speech might be defined as something you say to someone else. However, talking in itself is not formal enough to be considered a speech. A speaker must organize ideas carefully so that random thoughts appear in a logical sequence. Organization and sequence differentiate a speech from a conversation.

Limiting the Topic of a Speech

Preparing a speech begins with selecting a topic—a difficult task. Begin with a general area of interest and choose a specific subject that will appeal to your audience. Do not try to cover too much. If the general topic is pollution control, isolate one part of that large field (e.g., industrial emissions) and let the part represent the whole.

Limiting the scope of a presentation prevents digression and vagueness. You can begin limiting by defining your purpose—information or persuasion. (Since speeches usually *tell* and not *ask*, inquiry is not a common type of speech.) Then analyze the audience's needs. (See Chapter 2 for a discussion of purpose and audience.) What do they know, and what do they want to know? What do you want them to know? The topic will be limited naturally by your own knowledge and experience. Remember the primary rule of public speaking: if you do not know what you are talking about, close your mouth!

The Three-Part Plan of Organization

Since a speech requires clear forward movement, begin with a thesis or topic statement that anticipates the conclusion you are trying to reach. Then provide supporting facts and arguments and end with a summary of major points. Putting a conclusive statement in the introduction will help clarify purpose immediately.

THE BEGINNING

Many speeches begin with an acknowledgment of the host and the occasion. This is appropriate and courteous, but digressive. The listener has to wait until the pleasantries are over before the "real" speech begins. Another way of beginning is to ask a rhetorical question, "Has anyone in this room ever experienced stage fright?" With a question like this, the audience is immediately engaged in a subject that affects them. This device is useful in establishing the two-way communication of question and response, but asking too many questions places the burden of answering on the audience. The wrong kind of question—"How many of you didn't want to be here today?" or "Do you really want lower taxes?"—could inspire the audience to think of the wrong answer.

Another way to begin a speech is to present the conclusion. If you state that nuclear power will save or destroy our nation, you will appeal to the audience's need for survival. Then you must prove the truth and validity of the statement. Many speakers like to keep their conclusions a secret, saving the surprise until the end, but speeches are not mystery fiction (usually). Stating the conclusion at the beginning of the speech arouses the audience's interest to see how such a bold statement can be proved.

After the introductory paragraph, give an example that will illustrate the topic. In other words, "call up a mental picture." A positive example will help bring people to your side: "A new dam has already saved three towns just like ours." A negative example will demonstrate the faults of the opposing position: "City council opposed the new dam, and now city hall is under water." When you use examples, be sure they are relevant and keep them brief at the beginning.

If a printed program or the person introducing you has not given your credentials, you may need to establish your own credibility at the outset. The best way to do this is to mention your name and title and then honestly and factually demonstrate a depth of knowledge. Do not say you are the world's leading authority on a subject; imply your authority by force of argument. You can mention in passing a title or responsibility to show your level of involvement: "As chairman of the committee on . . . I have personally reported to the president that . . . ." You can establish credibility by demonstrating knowledge and relating experience.

Sometimes at the end of the introduction it is effective to review the relevance of the topic, mentioning the background, current situation, and immediate effect on the audience. This kind of general summary provides a conclusion to the introductory section and a transition to the body of the speech.

The partition statement (brief explanation of topics), considered essential by classical orators, is still helpful. Here, you can list briefly the topics you will cover or the arguments you will propose. If introduced like a shopping list, the partition statement will sound mechanical: "In this speech I will cover four topics—solar energy, hydroelectric energy, oil energy, and coal energy." A better statement integrates the four items within one sentence that can serve as a transition to the next section: "Of the four most important energy sources— solar, hydroelectric, oil, and coal—oil deserves our immediate attention because of the current oil crisis." The partition statement may come at the end of the introductory section or it may begin the body of the speech. Wherever you use it, the audience will appreciate hearing a verbal outline. An outlined speech is easier to follow and easier to believe because the organization shows planning.

THE BODY

After the introduction and the partition statement, begin to present the argument. Even an informative speech is an "argument" in a way because it must present facts and evidence in a logical sequence. If you use deductive logic, move from a general premise to a limiting minor premise and a conclusion that follows from the premises. Inductive logic requires a list of specific statements leading to a general conclusion. (See Chapter 3 for a discussion of logic.)

The organization of the speech's middle section may take one of many forms: historical (past to present); sequential (cause/effect, comparison/ contrast); or categorical (geographical relationships/natural divisions). These methods of organization are applicable to informative or persuasive speeches. The informative speech needs to show a logical progression; the persuasive speech needs to draw a conclusion from a sequence of facts.

Following are two brief outlines of the body emphasizing an informative speech and a persuasive speech.

INFORMATIVE SPEECH

STATUS OF DUPLICATED HOSPITAL SERVICES IN THE
METROPOLITAN AREA

I.   Introduction—Definition of Service Duplication

II. Body
     A. Hospitals Included

B. Where Services Are Duplicated
C. Cost of Duplication

III. Potential Areas of Consolidation

PROPOSAL TO ELIMINATE DUPLICATE HOSPITAL SERVICES
IN THE METROPOLITAN AREA

I. Introduction—Statement of Problem

II. Body
A. Hospitals Included
B. Where Services Are Duplicated
C. Cost of Duplication
D. How Services Can Be Distributed
E. Potential Savings
1. Money
2. People
F. Visualization of Results of Consolidation

III. Conclusion—Action Needed to Implement Plan

In either type of speech, the body should include as much support as necessary to state—but not to overstate—the situation. Be specific: list accurate figures and cite authorities; mention the negative arguments but *emphasize* the positive. Test logic by answering the *how-and-why* questions raised by your assertions, then balance each argument or section to give equal emphasis to supporting points. Eliminate the irrelevant and digressive, but use examples that illustrate your point, preferably ones in which you are directly involved. Plan transitions that summarize one point and lead naturally to the next topic. Finally, before concluding, review the organizational plan to see if you have articulated all relevant points.

THE CONCLUSION

To some speakers the conclusion is a relief: "Only a few more sentences and the speech will be over." If the speaker thinks this, the audience will be even more relieved when the speaker's mouth finally closes. A conclusion should be memorable, not perfunctory.

If your final words are "Well, I guess that's about all I have to say," the audience will remember that you had not organized your speech well enough to say something important. Use the conclusion to synthesize and reinforce.

The conclusion is a little speech in itself. In fact, if you were asked to prepare a thirty-minute speech and then told at the last second to cut the speech to five minutes, the conclusion should contain everything you want the audience to know. As with the introduction, you can begin with a statement or question: "Duplicating hospital services is expensive" or "How will consolidating hospital services work?" Then give a summary of the major points in one or two sentences. "Of the six major hospitals, all have the same emergency services, but only two need to maintain 'CAT scan' equipment to serve the public efficiently. These two hospitals can therefore expand neurological services while the other four can use their savings to expand emergency services."

In an informative speech, summarize the main points and highlight significant data. In a persuasive speech, conclude with an appraisal of the present and a visualization of the future: "The lives of two people were lost today because none of our hospitals could afford the latest brain-scan equipment. If we consolidate neurological services at University Hospital, we can treat brain injuries effectively, while making more money and more beds available for general emergency services at other hospitals." The final statement should be memorable: "Community cooperation works; it might even save your life." The approach to an audience should be concrete. You are an individual telling other individuals how they can benefit from what you have told them.

Other Plans of Organization

The three-part approach is a natural organization for a speech; we are accustomed by myth and logic to believe in the power of three. However, there are other ways to organize speeches or at least to expand on the basic "trinity."

CICERONIAN ORATORY

Cicero was one of the world's most successful orators. Although he believed in the value of being extemporaneous (or appearing to be so) and of the need to be flexible in organization, he codified a system of argumentation for political and judicial speeches. In the essay, "*De Orationis*" ("On Oratory"), he outlined the seven parts of an effective speech.

   I   *Exordium*—A concise introduction appealing to the audience's self-interest

  II *Partition*—Major topics "set briefly forth"

 III *Narrative*—Background and current situation

 IV *Confirmation*—Supporting facts and authorities

  V *Refutation*—Challenge to counterarguments

VI   *Digression*—Example supporting main thesis

VII   *Peroration*—Summary and conclusion

For Cicero and other rhetoricians a speech without these elements was inconclusive and therefore unsuccessful. Most three-part speeches with a beginning, middle, and end contain Cicero's seven elements:

Part I—Exordium, narrative, partition

Part II—Confirmation, refutation, digression

Part III—Peroration

For those who speak often, expanding the three into seven may help achieve a complete and logical organization.

STRATEGY FOR PERSUASION

Classical oratory has influenced modern speakers who have adapted old forms to their own personalities and the needs of the audience. Modern rhetoricians like John Dewey and Alan H. Monroe, have developed a sequence of persuasion that attempts to move an audience to act.[1] The classical form within the sequence is easy to identify; the additions appeal to the audience's needs, sympathy, and self-interest.

I   There Is a Problem—State the problem clearly in terms the audience will understand.

II   It Is *Your* Problem—Although everyone is affected by the problem, the individuals in the audience are especially involved because they have experienced the problem and can help solve it.

III   Background of Problem—Tell the audience things they know, but add details they might not know in order to establish your own credibility.

IV   Criteria for Solving Problem—Establish specific needs that must be met if the solution is to be valid.

V   Possible Solutions—List major relevant solutions, including some you might not favor. Establish common ground, if any.

VI   Best Solution—Introduce your own solution, showing that it satisfies the general criteria for solving the problem but also showing that it will be more effective than other proposals because it is comprehensive.

---

[1] Monroe's "motivated sequence," can be found in Douglas Ehninger, Alan H. Monroe, and Bruce E. Gronbeck, *Principles and Types of Speech Communication,* 8th ed. (Glenville, IL: Scott, Foresman), 1978. The variation on Dewey and Monroe presented here has been developed by David Wolford.

VII   Action Step[2]—Tell the audience that since your solution is valid, they should take immediate action to solve a serious problem.

VIII   Visualization—Call up a mental picture of what you and the audience can achieve together with your solution. Be specific and vivid.

IX   Recommendation—Make a specific recommendation with dates and times for action.

X   Conclusion—Leave the audience with the sense that they know how to solve the problem. Then challenge them: if they can solve a serious problem now, why wait to take action?

Like any device, this sequence of persuasion can be mechanical. Yet it also can offer a ready-made outline for a speech on a problem that must be solved. The model can be modified and adapted to many situations requiring workable solutions. Here is an example of a problem faced by many residents of many urban areas.

Our town smells![1] You know it smells because you have to walk through the streets every day.[2] The day the new factory opened, the town began to smell.[3] Now we must find a way to eliminate the plant's waste products without destroying the town's economy.[4]

We could demand that the plant close altogether, make them install a waste recycling system, or limit operation time to night when we're indoors.[5] Or we could recommend that they install a cheaper, modified filter system that would reduce the smelly gases to a solid waste that can be buried.[6]

We have lived with this problem too long; and, since there is a workable solution—a modified filter system—we should present our proposal to the company.[7] If we do act, think about how nice it will be to look at a blue sky without soot and to smell blossoms instead of sulfur.[8] Add your name to the list of those who will meet with company representatives next Wednesday.[9] Together we can make our town beautiful again.[10]

---

[1] There is a problem.
[2] It is your problem.
[3] Background of problem.
[4] Criteria for solving problem.
[5] Possible solutions.
[6] Best solution.
[7] Action step.
[8] Visualization.
[9] Recommendation.
[10] Conclusion.

---

[2] In Monroe's "sequence," the visualization step precedes the action step: attention, need, satisfaction, visualization, action.

Exercises

1   Select a simple topic (a process, a product, a place) and make an outline for a three-point speech. After listing the three important points, reorganize the outline to make the conclusion the introduction.

2   Choose a general topic (pollution, business recession, investment) and prepare an outline for an informative speech on the topic. Analyze the major categories and make an outline for a speech on one of them. Include a clear introduction, supporting facts, and a conclusion that summarizes the ideas contained in the introduction and body.

3   Plan a persuasive speech on an important topic (giving blood, correcting an injustice, trying something new). Use the "motivating sequence" as your outline.

4   Find the test of an important speech. (See the semimonthly publication, *Vital Speeches of the Day.*) Make an outline of the speech and determine its purpose. Note the introduction, partition statement (if any), supporting facts, examples, and conclusion.

Chapter 12

Preparation and Rehearsal

Preparation

After limiting your topic and organizing your ideas, you will need to find the facts that prove your point and give you credibility. Speeches, as well as written documents, contain historical data, a report of current activity, definition of terms, description of a process, and statistics including financial information. Do not use your memory to assemble all this information. Formulate a research plan and carry it out. (See Chapter 2.)

MANUSCRIPT OR NOTES

Once initial research and organization are complete (you will have to continue adding details and refining organization), you will be ready to prepare your manuscript or notes. If you plan to read your speech, prepare a cleanly typed manuscript with enough space and margins to accommodate last-minute notes. If you use a large typeface, find one that will distinguish between capitals and lowercase so that you can see where sentences stop and begin.

If you plan to speak from an outline, you can either type your outlined notes on 8½- by 11-inch sheets of paper (legal size is too cumbersome) or transfer the outline to index cards. If the complete outline is on one or two sheets of paper, you will find it easier to keep your place when speaking, but remember to arrange for a lectern. Index cards, properly numbered, give you freedom. You can hold them in one hand or slide them from one pile to another. Do not put too little information on one card because mechanically changing cards with each point can annoy an audience and cause you to concentrate on the cards instead of the speech.

Whatever method you use, expand the topic outline to include key sentences and other notations. You might wish to write out the introduction and the conclusion, as well as topic sentences and transitions. Perhaps a word or phrase to remind you of an example will keep you from straying from the main point. However, do not write the whole speech, word for word on cards. If you want to read the speech, use sheets for paper.

Mark your notes for emphasis and pauses, with different colors for different purposes. For example, use one color for emphasis (perhaps red), another for breath, and a third for a hand gesture or special physical movement. A clearly marked manuscript is a road map to guide you from beginning to end. Speakers are often frightened about getting lost; a clear, well-prepared manuscript or set of notes will remove one of the fears of speaking.

VISUAL AIDS

After the manuscript is ready, prepare visual aids if you need them. (See Chapter 14). First, look at the outline to see where visual representation will help: lists, comparisons, illustrations, etc. Then make a rough draft of the visual aids, being as complete as possible. Use visual aids only to illustrate a point, not to tell the whole story. You must control the number and kinds of visual aids so that they do not dominate the speech. Remember, instead of *showing* pictures, you may find "calling up mental pictures" more effective because you and the audience are involved together. Showing too many visuals distracts the audience and, if the material is complex, may cause them to interpret the data for themselves.

Rehearsal

Rehearsal is an important step in the process of preparing to speak. For the first rehearsal, find the room where you will be giving your speech or presentation. If this is not possible, choose a space that will enable you to set up the physical environment the way you want it. You will need at the very least a standing lectern or a table with a half lectern. Place yourself at the front of an imagined audience and read all your notes aloud, pausing to mark problem passages and places where additional information is needed. When you hear your own words for the first time, you will become an audience, listening for vagueness and coherence. Time the first rehearsal so that you will know if you are speaking too quickly or too slowly or if you have prepared too much or too little. Since the first rehearsal is more for judging pace, organization, and content than for delivery, you do not need to use an audio or video recorder. Recording will be helpful later in polishing your delivery.

After the first run-through, immediately begin to revise. Leave at least a day for revision and be prepared to reorganize your entire speech if necessary. Since the facts will remain the same, you will not have to start over completely. Emphasis and examples may change, however. Be prepared to work hard on the revision; the first version should not be the last version if you want your presentation to be polished.

The second rehearsal should approximate the real speaking situation. If you can rehearse in the room scheduled for your speech, you can gain confidence by knowing the physical surroundings and the equipment. In any case, rehearse with an audio recorder, video playback system, or a few friends. You need the feedback provided by a recording or personal evaluation because you are not the best judge of the way you look or sound to others. A video system is especially helpful in showing your bad and *good* points. Most of us look better than we think we do.

As you rehearse, concentrate on enunciation, voice projection, and body movement. Watch and listen to yourself as you speak, and mark your manuscript for adjustments. Time your presentation accurately: the final presentation should not vary much in length and content from the second rehearsal.

At the end of the second rehearsal, make a list of the problems you will have to solve—words you trip over, weak transitions, integration of visual aids, wordiness, or distracting physical movement. Mark your manuscript again (perhaps using a fresh copy to avoid messiness) and read aloud only the new changes you have made. You are then ready for the third rehearsal.

The third rehearsal combines the major structural changes and the detailed changes in transitions and delivery. After this, there is not much else you can do. You will know how you look and sound, and you will be able to anticipate your audience's response to your logic.

The number of additional rehearsals you need is up to you. Rehearse as much as needed to become completely comfortable with your presentation. If you continue rehearsing, work on pronunciation, emphasis, breathing, pauses, gestures, and the ease with which you can use visual aids. Continue to use an audio or video recorder so that you can judge each new rehearsal against the previous ones. But do not rehearse too much or you will overprepare and lose any sense of spontaneity. When you become bored with rehearsing, you are in danger of boring the audience with a presentation that sounds like a recording.

Above all, become enthusiastic. In the first rehearsal, you have to concentrate on saying everything for the first time. In subsequent rehearsals, put yourself into the speech. Speak with authority and show that you believe your own words by emphasizing important points and by looking your imagined audience straight in their collective eye and urging them to listen and believe. You do not have to be an actor, but you should underscore your words with enthusiasm. Project your personality convincingly, matching force of presentation with conviction of meaning.

CHECKLIST FOR REHEARSING

1 *Preparation.* Prepare notes (or manuscript) and visual aids in a clean, easy-to-read form.

2 *First Rehearsal.* Give the presentation without timing it. Listen for vagueness and coherence. Mark difficult passages.

3 *Revision.* Revise to tighten organization, to delete digressions, and to add new facts where necessary.

4 *Second Rehearsal.* If possible, go to the room where you will be speaking. Decide what type of lectern and visual apparatus you will need. Use an audio or video recorder or an informal audience so you can receive feedback from your rehearsal. Time the presentation.

5 *Third Rehearsal.* Repeat the presentation until you become thoroughly comfortable with it and with your surroundings. Anticipate audience response.

Exercises

1 Make an outline of a presentation. Experiment with several formats: 3- by 5-inch cards; 4- by 6-inch cards; 8½- by 11-inch paper. Determine which format will allow you to become comfortable as you give your presentation.

2 If your speech is written out, read the manuscript into a tape recorder, emphasizing diction and vocal variety. If you do not have a written speech, read a paragraph from a book. Practice until you become comfortable with the material.

3 Prepare a three-point speech that is not written out word for word. Rehearse the speech without recording it, then present the speech to a live audience or to an audio or video recorder. Evaluate organization and clarity.

4 In the next presentation you attend, determine whether the speaker was aware of the physical surroundings and the needs of the audience to see and hear. Evaluate the smoothness of the presentation.

Chapter 13

Techniques of Delivery

Controlling Stage Fright

CAUSES AND EFFECTS

"Has anyone ever experienced stage fright?" When an audience hears this question, nearly every hand will shoot up. When asked, "Why are you afraid?" a brave person who can find a voice will answer, "Because I do not want to make a fool of myself. And I do not want to go through the pain of being challenged by a large audience. I can deal with five or six people, but no more than that."

People are afraid of public speaking because they do not understand the process, and they do not understand their fears. Stage fright is caused by a lack of confidence, the fear of the unknown, and a distrust of crowds whose anonymity is threatening. The effects of these fears are mostly negative, but they can be positive if a speaker learns to understand the causes and the remedies.

The physical effects of stage fright vary—pounding heart, dry mouth, tight muscles, shaking knees, butterflies, sweat rashes, and stomach upsets. Like other disorders caused by anxiety, the effects are real but controllable if the anxieties are reduced. For some, a certain amount of nervousness is helpful because it forces better preparation and awareness of the audience. To control your nerves, prepare as well as you can, leaving nothing to chance.

Antidotes

PREPARATION

The problems associated with stage fright may sound acute (especially to first-time speakers), but remedies exist. The best antidotes to stage fright are adequate research, preparation, and rehearsal. If you are enthusiastic about your message and confident of its organization, you can concentrate on the act of communicating with the audience. With adequate preparation, you can control the situation because you are active and the audience is passive. For them to react at all, they need to listen to what you have to say. If you approach them with sound logic and self-confidence, the audience will respect and believe you.

Still, just before a speech begins, stage fright can transform butterflies into scorpions. If your heart pounds, let it. Heart pounding is a way your body releases tension, and you will not keel over as a result. Take enough breaths to maintain sufficient oxygen in your bloodstream; consciously relax your muscles by opening and closing your hands, letting your arms dangle, and dropping your shoulders to avoid hunching over.

Another method of controlling stage fright has various names, which can be reduced to, "Think good thoughts." Do not imagine yourself tripping on the way to the lectern, mixing up your cards, or losing your voice in the middle of a sentence. Instead, think of something relaxing—lying on the sand, sailing, gardening. Deflecting your thoughts from the negative to the positive can reduce anxiety and its physical manifestations.

EYE CONTACT

Adequate preparation and techniques of relaxation can help before you begin speaking. The most effective way to control stage fright while you are speaking is to maintain eye contact with the individuals who make up the audience. Looking people straight in the eye helps take your mind off yourself and makes you devote attention to your listeners.

Before you walk up to the lectern, locate some people in the audience who look receptive—perhaps some friends, a person who seems to be smiling, or if it is a large audience, someone with colorful clothes. Use that person as a point of focus. When you finally walk up to the lectern, do not start speaking immediately. Locate your first focus point and then find other receptive faces, one on each side of you, one in the middle, and one in the back. By identifying four or five people who look interested, you already have begun to separate the mass into a group of individuals.

When you utter your first words, speak directly to one person. Then begin to move your eyes around the room, not mechanically but naturally so you will not look like a puppet. Do not look between individuals or up to the ceiling where people might think you have pasted your notes. Do not concentrate too long on the eyes of one person because people who are stared at become very uncomfortable and because you might lose your place. Move your eyes around the room and speak to individuals. You cannot speak to more than one person at a time, but while you are speaking and your listener is responding, the rest of the audience is eavesdropping and waiting for you to contact them. They will listen attentively because they know that each member of the audience is receiving individual attention.

Even a listener with a scowl deserves at least a glance. It is not necessary to start talking to an apparently unfriendly person, but at some time during the presentation face that person with the conviction that you know what you are doing. You cannot please everyone, but as a speaker you must approach everyone. If you take your mind off your anxieties and concentrate on the individuals in the audience, you will learn to control stage fright.

Eliminating stage fright altogether may not be possible or necessary. Before every speech, you should review a mental or written checklist of the remedies for stage fright.

CHECKLIST FOR CONTROLLING STAGE FRIGHT

1   Know what you are going to say.

2   Know your audience.

3   Imagine yourself in a comfortable situation.

4   Breathe.

5   Relax your muscles.

6   Establish eye contact.

7   Maintain enthusiasm.

Each time you speak you will become more familiar with the process itself and with the methods that will make you an effective communicator. More than anything else, experience is the best way to control stage fright. Nevertheless, you can use your apprehension to make you prepare adequately and to learn more about your audience and your own strengths as a speaker. With self-confidence and enthusiasm, you and the individuals in the audience should enjoy the speech.

Preparing to Speak

Adequate preparation for a speech means knowing as much as you can about the speaking situation. As soon as you accept the invitation or assignment, contact one person who can answer questions and make physical arrangements. You need to rely on someone who knows the exact location of the presentation, the size and makeup of the audience, and the kind of equipment available. When requesting equipment, leave nothing to chance. If you need a blackboard, ask for chalk and an eraser as well; if you need an overhead projector, ask for a screen, too.

When you arrive at the site of your presentation, go immediately to the room, check the setup, and test all equipment. It is your responsibility to make sure that everything is working to your satisfaction. "Murphy's Law" applies with a vengeance to speaking situations, but at least you can try to prevent trouble.

While you are setting up the room, you will probably be speaking with your host and some early arrivals. Project your personality immediately as a person who will tell them something they need to know. Learn as many names as you can, and create a rapport so that you can establish eye contact when the speech begins.

If you speak after a meal, avoid milk, creamy sauces, ice cream, or other foods that could coat your vocal cords. Drink hot coffee or tea to dilute the phlegm that might have gathered. Do not drink alcohol to relax yourself. For many people, alcohol will cause a loss of self-control. It is embarrassing to stand in front of an audience sweating and "wixing mords."

Warm up your voice by speaking out loud just before you begin. Use polite conversation to begin projecting your voice as if you were speaking to a large audience. If no one is around (and if no one can hear you), hum. Vibrations of the vocal cords will also help loosen phlegm.

Since people are quick to catch physical idiosyncracies, check your appearance before speaking. Comb your hair, zip zippers, and button buttons— be aware of how you look. A good appearance shows that you want to make a positive impression on an audience.

When it is time to begin speaking, walk slowly to the lectern. Place your notes in a convenient, prearranged spot, and then pause for a second or two to look around the audience and find a friendly face. Take a deep but unobtrusive breath, and speak your first words with authority. Begin with an attention-getting statement that will immediately involve your audience. Continue to speak with enthusiasm, summarizing main points and offering clear transitions and a conclusion that reminds the audience of your first words. If the conclusion echoes the introduction and the internal structure is coherent, the audience will recognize a well-organized speech.

Memorable Speakers

Learning good delivery skills requires concentration. Begin by asking the common questions: What do I do with my hands? How do I stand? How can I stop saying, "Uh?" Since it is easier to see the mistakes others make, look critically at speakers, noticing both the distractions and the effective techniques. Although the content of a speech is always more important than the delivery, good speakers use effective delivery to emphasize and clarify meaning. Ineffective speakers have not *planned* their delivery. The following speakers are examples of those whose words are lost forever but whose delivery is immortalized.

THE CHANGE-MAKER

Jingling change or keys is the noisiest of distractions. This speaker forgot that lesson when he did not put his change in hs briefcase. As soon as he was introduced, he put his left hand in his pocket and for twenty minutes jingled his coins noisily. He seemed to be comfortable and calm, but the audience was relieved when he finally sat down.

THE GRAND PIANIST

This speaker used both hands for all his gestures. He used them so often, it looked like he was practicing the piano. His hands were almost begging the audience to concentrate more on the gestures than on the meaning of the speech.

THE HUNCHBACK

Tall people often seem to believe that the ceiling is an inch above their heads or that they must speak down into the microphone instead of out of the audience. One very tall speaker began by standing perfectly straight for his introduction, and then for the rest of the speech he rested his left elbow on the lectern, diminishing his stature and his credibility.

THE "UH"-SAYER

One-hundred twenty-one "uh's" in ten minutes may be a world's record. This speaker could not listen to himself, and the audience could not listen to the speech. He later saw a videotape of his speech and found that every time he paused he said "Uh." The next time he spoke, he kept his mouth shut until he started a new sentence, reducing the number of "uh's" to three.

THE SNOWY EGRET

She came from Washington with a briefcase and white snow boots, which she did not remove. For nearly half an hour she stood on one foot with the other extended behind her. She had to grip the lectern to keep from falling over. She wavered occasionally.

THE POLKA-DOT FLAG

This speaker waved herself in front of the audience. She began by speaking very slowly, but as she continued, she picked up speed and ran her words together without pause so that the audience could not distinguish one point from the other. She became so frantic that her face and neck (she was wearing a low-cut blouse) got blotchy. Finally, she exhaled and stopped. Her problem was that she had forgotten to breathe. Breathing is helpful. It provides oxygen to the bloodstream and helps prevent polka dots.

Many other strange beings appear in the public forum. They should be an example, not to follow but to show us ourselves. Do you wander, crouch, rock, or utter strange noises while you speak? If you yourself are offended by such obvious distractions, you have to expect those watching you to be offended, causing them to remember *how* you spoke rather than *what* you said.

Techniques of Delivery

Techniques of delivery can be learned. Effective speaking blends content and delivery, and the two reinforce each other. Attempt to be natural when you speak; to do so, remember a list of techniques that will give you confidence.

POSTURE

Stand straight, with head erect. Keep both feet on the ground, with one slightly ahead of the other to prevent rocking from side to side and to make it possible to pivot. Keep your back straight and shoulders parallel to the ground. Stand erect but not stiff.

BREATHING

Normal breathing may not be enough to project your voice adequately. Always mark your notes or manuscript at places where pausing and breathing will help you maintain a steady pace and voice level. When pausing, breathe through your nose to avoid drying out your month. Do not sniff, but instead suck the air into the back of your throat and fill up your lungs. As your chest cavity expands, the diaphragm will flatten, and then as you exhale, the diaphragm will force the air out of the lungs, much like a bellows.[1] If you exhale slowly and with a controlled rhythm, you will have enough breath to sustain and project your vocal tone.

---

[1] For a detailed description of correct breathing and the use of the diaphragm, see Virgil A. Anderson, *Training the Speaking Voice* (New York: Oxford University Press, 1977), p. 38.

BODY

Body movement prevents you from looking stiff and uncomfortable. When speaking behind a lectern, move unobtrusively one or two feet to each side—if you feel the need to change positions. If you choose to move in front of the lectern or table, do not sit down, and do not wander aimlessly or you will appear absent-minded and out of control. You can be informal without slouching or dangling your legs. If you use a blackboard or screen, stand so that you can pivot between audience and screen. Always use your body to emphasize meaning. Do not let thoughtless movement intrude on the overall effectiveness of your speech.

HANDS

Hands sometimes seem independent of the body. If you have a lectern, place your hands on top, palms down. Clenched fists make you look nervous. Do not grip the lectern or push it from you. Some lecterns are on wheels; they are especially dangerous at the edge of a stage. Keeping your hands on the lectern will enable you to lift them only a short distance for an appropriate gesture.

Use hand gestures to emphasize points—strong beliefs, key words, questions, conclusions. Avoid pointing fingers at the audience; instead open your hand as a gesture of including your listeners. One-handed gestures underline meaning. Two-handed gestures can make you look as though you are trying to talk with your hands.

If you do not have a lectern, stand with both hands at your side. Do not place both hands behind you in the "parade rest" position. If you keep your hands behind you for a long time, you will look like you have no arms. Also, do not place your hands in the "fig leaf" position or hide them in your pockets. Do not clasp your hands together, and above all do not play with chalk, the insidious paper clip, or the collapsible pointer. Your hands are a part of your body; learn to control them so that they can help support your meaning and not distract the audience.

VOICE

When a person first hears himself on tape, the reaction is usually, "I sound awful." We do not sound "awful," just different from the voices coming from the mouths of others. After all, when we hear ourselves, our ears are behind the mouth, and we cannot pick up the natural resonance of our voice. Listeners usually make no judgment on voice quality unless it is especially raucous or raspy. However, they do notice diction, inflection, and variety of tone. If you listen to yourself and others carefully, you can train yourself to correct deficiencies in your voice.

First, be conscious of enunciation. Pronounce all syllables distinctly (dis*tinct*ly). Concentrate on internal dental sounds (*d* and *t*). Do not drop g's from the *ing* suffix. If you have a regional or foreign accent, do not try to change just to please the audience. If you speak at an even pace and with clear diction, the audience will concentrate on what you say and not how you say it.

Second, project your voice to the back of the room. You do not need to yell, especially because yelling irritates the vocal cords. However, you can "throw" or project your voice to everyone if you stand and breathe properly, pronounce words clearly, and speak with intensity. Even if you want to speak softly, you can lower the volume without decreasing the intensity.

Remember that you "owe" your voice to every individual in the audience. If you normally speak softly (perhaps so as not to offend or be noticed), modulate your voice. You will not change your personality if you speak so that everyone can hear. Likewise, if you usually bellow (perhaps so that everyone will notice and approve of you), decrease the volume and let the audience listen to meaning rather than sound. A good exercise for any speaker is to pick a short paragraph from a book and record it. Read it first with your natural volume, then speak softly but with intensity, and finally say it as loudly as you can without yelling. Be your own audience, and judge which sound is best, adjusting your voice accordingly the next time you speak. Soft- or loud-spoken people do not undergo a personality change if they modulate and project their voices properly.

Third, speak with a variety of sentence patterns. If all sentences are the same length with the same structure, you will sound dull. You will sound monotonous. You will sound bored. And you will sound boring. As you vary sentence structure, also vary emphasis within each sentence. Mark adjectives, nouns, or verbs that convey key ideas, and change your tone when you reach those ideas. Listen to how you conclude sentences. If you drop your voice at the end, all sentences will begin to sound alike. To achieve vocal variety, mark your manuscript: underline *important* words, use an accent mark to emphasize certain syllables, insert an upward arrow to show continuation, and add a downward arrow to signify a conclusion. Or devise your own system of notation. All sentences are not written alike, and they do not have to sound alike.

RELATIONSHIP TO AUDIENCE

The speaker must always maintain an unobstructed line of sight with the audience. Nothing should come between the speaker's eyes and the eyes of every listener. Adjust the microphone so that it is below your mouth and you can look over it. Avoid using half-glasses because they dissect your eyeballs and prevent the audience from looking directly at you.

If you use an overhead projector, find a table low enough so that the lense does not become a barrier but high enough so that you do not need to hunch over. With overhead transparencies you can speak from the slides without referring to the screen, maintaining a direct line of sight between you and the audience.

When using a screen, blackboard, or easel, establish a triangle by stepping aside. You may wish to consult the screen or board, but never turn your back on the audience to write or talk. Always leave open the possibility of eye contact and maintain an unobstructed view of the visuals.

SUMMARIES

Let your audience know where you are in your speech at all times. Begin with an introduction that is clear and to the point (it might have been your conclusion at one time). Include internal summaries of what you have covered and provide transitions to what remains. You might say something like, "The subject of delivery, my final point, is directly related to the first two topics, organization and stage fright." As you approach a transition, pause and breathe as a physical sign that you have finished one section and are about to move to another. Use your body and hands to signify a transition. Step back at a natural break, step up to show informality or intimacy, use an upward hand gesture to underline continuing action and a downward movement to signify determination and conclusion.

Deliver your conclusion emphatically and with a downward cadence to your voice. You can afford to be slightly dramatic because your last words should be memorable. Do not say, "Well, I guess that's about all I have to say, so if there are any questions, I'll be happy to sit down and answer them." Instead, end with a strong entreaty to action or an apt quotation that succinctly summarizes your speech.

Whenever you speak, keep in mind the techniques that will help you prepare and communicate your message.

CHECKLIST FOR GIVING A SPEECH

1   As you prepare
    a   Find out the exact location of the building, room, and time scheduled for your speech.
    b   Find out who will attend and how much you can expect them to know about your subject.
    c   Tell your contact what equipment you will need: microphones; slide, movie, or overhead projectors; easel or blackboard.

2   When you arrive
    a   Check room setup.
    b   Test equipment and acoustics.
    c   Greet your host and others who will be listening to you.

3   Before you speak
    a   Avoid alcohol and food that could coat your vocal cords.
    b   Warm up your voice. Try to speak out loud just before your presentation begins. If no one is nearby, hum.
    c   Comb your hair and straighten your clothes.

4 When you begin
    a Walk slowly to the lectern, place your manuscript or notes in a convenient spot.
    b Pause before you begin. Size up the audience and find some friendly faces.
    c Begin with a clear attention-getting statement.

5 As you speak
    a Keep your audience aware of the message you are communicating. Summarize main points and provide clear transitions.
    b Stand straight and tall. Do not rock.
    c Use gestures for emphasis, not to distract.
    d Establish eye contact all over the room. Speak to individuals, not to everyone at the same time.
    e Vary the length of sentences, and modulate your voice speech patterns.
    f Breathe properly in order to support your voice. Project your voice so that everyone can hear you. Mark your notes with signs to breathe, pause, or emphasize.
    g Conclude with a strong summary statement that will remind the audience of your message.

Although this checklist will help you prepare for a formal speech, you can use the suggestions for other types of speaking. For example, if you are suddenly called on to give an impromptu account of your department's recent achievements and future plans, you should run through your own checklist before speaking.

1 Organization
    a Conclusion
    b Facts
    c Analysis

2 Delivery
    a Eye contact
    b Body
    c Voice

With your goal and facts in mind and with self-awareness of voice and gestures, you should be able to give a brief speech. In fact, these checklists will help you prepare for any type of communication: interpersonal, individual, and group.

Exercises

1 Read a paragraph out loud in front of a long mirror. Look up as often as possible and analyze your facial movements, hand gestures, and feet. After practicing by yourself, speak to a small audience or in front of a video recorder.

2 To practice proper breathing, try to count to fifty with one breath. Do not let out too much air for the first ten digits and stop before you run out of breath. Speak rhythmically, sustaining an even tone of voice.

3 To practice diction and projection, read a paragraph out loud into a tape recorder. Enunciate clearly, achieving vocal variety by emphasizing important words. After practicing for smoothness, vary the volume. Read the paragraph again in your normal tone. Then, read it as loudly as you can without yelling and irritating your vocal cords. Finally, read as softly as you can but with good breath control in order to project clearly.

4 Write an outline for a three-point speech. Create a conclusion that will summarize the entire speech and then practice delivering the summary and conclusion. Concentrate on the final sentence, and give the audience something positive to remember.

Chapter 14

Using Visual Aids

Definition

The important part of the term *visual aids* is the word *aid*. Graphic material supports a presentation by illustrating important ideas and by allowing the audience to see as well as to hear. However, the speaker must control the numbers and kinds of visual aids so that they do not dominate the presentation. Visual aids show the audience data, relationships, and conclusions.

Types

The most common types of visual aids fall into two general categories: words and illustrations. A third category, objects, is not used very often because the actual object is often difficult to bring to a podium. Nevertheless, when explaining the development of something like a mechanical hand, the speaker will not have to make the audience imagine the object if it is there for them to see. Illustrations represent objects, and words call up mental pictures.

WORDS

Words lead the audience through a logical progression of ideas. When the visual aids present *only* words, however, the audience will do the speaker's job by

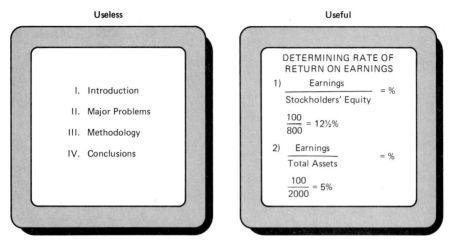

Figure 14-1   "Word visuals."

reading the text. Or, worse, the speaker will offend an audience by reading the text to them. Such useless visuals present outlines whose only purpose is to remind the speaker of what the presentation's sequence should be. This type of visual aid is neither important nor an aid to understanding. Other types of visual aids can help the audience understand a sequence of ideas by mixing words and numbers in a very clear sequence that shows a step-by-step development. The speaker and the visual both do the necessary work to instruct the listener.

ILLUSTRATIONS

Photographs.   Pictures show size, depth, color, and relationship to surroundings. Too many pictures, however, will turn a speech into a movie with subtitles.

Drawings.   Drawings can be helpful to illustrate technical details or processes. For audiences used to reading mechanical plans, drawings save the time of detailed explanations.

Tables.   If tables show too much they can be difficult to comprehend. Simple data with important information underlined or circled will help the audience understand what the table is supposed to demonstrate.

Graphs.   Graphs demonstrate relationships and trends. In oral presentations, graphic material should be simple because the viewer must assimilate the information quickly while listening to the speaker. In a written report, the reader has time to study the data. Among the most useful types of graphs are the bar graph, line graph, and pie chart. (See Chapter 7 for examples.) Flow charts and organizational charts also help clarify complex information.

Figure 14-2   Sample drawing for a visual aid.

Preparation

Two simple rules govern the use of visual aids: (1) make them easy to understand, and (2) do not use too many. When preparing visuals, concentrate on one subject for each picture or drawing. Use only relevant materials such as current data, unusual developments, or relationships of categories that are alike. After deciding on the type of material you wish to show, make a rough copy that includes all pertinent information. Before sending the rough copy to an artist or redoing it yourself, check for accuracy (correct the spelling and verify all numbers) and consistency. When all rough drafts have been completed, compare them with each other for consistency and determine which visuals should be added or deleted.

Visuals should improve meaning and not intrude on the structure of the argument. Visual aids should be visible for at least as long as it takes an audience to understand the material. Since it will take a minute and a half or more to explain even a simple visual, two in five minutes is the most an audience will be able to absorb. Even this figure is not a rule, however, because twelve visual aids in thirty minutes might be too many, making the visuals more important than the words.

Be careful not to use too few. If you put all your ideas on one visual, you will probably have to read the material to the audience. If you have only one visual aid in a presentation, the material should be important enough to warrant intruding on the smoothness of the delivery of the words. (*Unveiling* a product by

Useless

	Nov.	Dec.	1983 Apr.	May.	Jun.	Jul.	Aug.	Sept.	Oct.	Nov.	Dec.	1981	1982	1983
Industrial Production...	134.9	135.2	142.6	144.4	146.4	149.7	151.8	153.8	155.0	156.1	156.9	150.9	138.6	147.7
%.................	-0.6	0.2	1.9	1.3	1.4	2.3	1.4	1.3	0.8	0.7	0.5	2.6	-8.1	6.5
% Year Ago..........	-7.8	-5.7	1.7	3.7	5.6	7.9	9.7	12.0	14.2	15.7	16.1			
Manufacturing.........	134.0	134.5	143.1	145.1	147.4	150.6	152.8	155.1	156.4	157.2	157.8	150.3	137.5	148.4
%.................	-0.7	0.4	1.9	1.4	1.6	2.2	1.5	1.5	0.8	0.5	0.4	2.4	-8.5	7.9
% Year Ago..........	-7.6	-5.3	3.2	5.2	7.0	9.1	10.7	13.1	15.9	17.3	17.3			
Durables.............	119.3	119.9	129.1	131.0	133.2	136.8	138.8	141.6	143.0	144.0	145.0	140.4	124.7	134.6
% SAAR.............	-9.5	6.2	30.1	19.2	22.1	37.7	19.0	27.1	12.5	8.7	8.7	2.7	-11.1	7.9
% Year Ago..........	-11.2	-8.7	1.9	3.9	6.1	8.7	11.1	14.7	18.9	20.7	20.9			
Nondurables..........	155.3	155.6	163.3	165.4	167.8	170.6	172.9	174.6	175.8	176.3	176.3	164.7	156.1	168.3
% SAAR.............	-6.7	2.3	21.2	16.6	18.9	22.0	17.4	12.5	8.6	3.5	0.0	2.2	-5.2	7.9
% Year Ago..........	-3.1	-1.1	4.6	6.7	8.0	9.6	10.2	11.4	12.5	13.5	13.3			
Stone, Clay & Glass(32).	127.3	125.4	138.3	139.2	141.7	145.8	147.9	151.7	151.9	153.9		148.1	128.3	
%.................	-0.6	-1.5	2.0	0.7	1.8	2.9	1.4	2.6	0.1	1.3		0.1	-13.3	
Primary Metals(33)......	63.6	63.5	83.1	84.9	84.8	85.5	87.5	90.6	95.1	92.0	91.1	107.7	75.1	85.6
%.................	-8.6	-0.2	2.3	2.2	-0.1	0.8	2.3	3.5	5.0	-3.3	-1.0	5.4	-30.3	13.9
Steel & Mill Prod(331).	47.7	49.2	68.5	70.1	69.2	71.9	75.9	79.5	86.3	82.4		102.3	62.2	
%.................	-11.5	3.1	-3.8	2.3	-1.3	3.9	5.6	4.7	8.6	-4.5		8.3	-39.2	
Iron & Steel Found(332)	50.8	40.5	62.9	64.1	61.9	68.8	73.3	67.9	74.5	72.7		88.8	59.2	
%.................	-2.5	-20.3	2.1	1.9	-3.4	11.1	6.5	-7.4	9.7	-2.4		3.1	-33.4	
Nonferrous Metals(333).	90.3	88.5	96.3	98.5	101.5	102.1	106.2	109.4	110.4	111.7		132.1	100.0	
%.................	0.8	-2.0	-0.6	2.3	3.0	0.6	4.0	3.0	0.9	1.2		1.0	-24.3	

Useful

Physician visits (Number per person)	1964	1976	1981
Total	4.6	4.9	4.6
Whites	4.7	4.9	4.6
Blacks	3.6	4.8	4.7
By family income*			
Less than $7,000	3.9	5.6	5.6
$7,000 to $9,999	4.2	4.8	4.9
$10,000 to $14,999	4.7	4.8	4.5
$15,000 to $24,999	4.8	4.9	4.5
$25,000 or more	5.2	4.9	4.4

*In 1981 dollars

Figure 14-3   Sample tables for a visual aid. (Source: top, Wharton Econometric Forecasting Associates. Bottom, *The New York Times.*)

showing it or a picture of it can be dramatic.) In most cases, however, using only one visual aid will cause the audience to question the need for something that could have been explained more easily than shown.

When all material is assembled—outlines, visual aids, projectors, easels— your preparation is complete. Before you begin rehearsing, reread your notes for organization and coherence, then number all cards, sheets, and visual aids. Finally, key the visual aids to the proper place on your notes. The more complete your physical preparation, the greater your confidence will be.

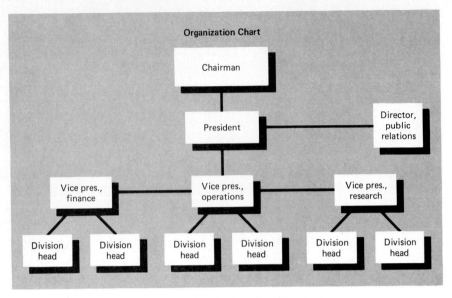

Figure 14-4   Sample chart for a visual aid.

Format

The term visual aids refers to many formats. Movies, videotapes, slide tapes, and filmstrips are all visual forms that are complete in themselves. In fact, speakers cannot usually interrupt these automatic types of presentations.

The more common types of visual aids used to support a presentation are overhead transparencies, 35-mm slides, easels, and blackboard.

OVERHEAD PROJECTOR

This machine projects images on plastic transparencies. It is useful because preparation is cheap and fast. If a graphic artist is unavailable, draw, print, or type (with a large typeface) the material and copy it on an automatic copy machine. Then, run the copy through a transparency maker, which will pick up the carbon and create a sharp image. Add color by using marking pens or self-sticking cellophane, or use color transparencies. Tape the finished transparency to a cardboard frame, labeling with a title, number, and directions for use—*this side up*! When using transparencies, turn the machine off if you are not showing anything, and do not keep a transparency on after you have stopped referring to it. The noise and glare will distract the audience.

35-MM SLIDES

Photographic slides convey a sharp image and a professional appearance. The danger of using slides is that the audience will not be able to see the speaker with the lights off and that the quantity and quality of slides might detract from the speaker.

EASEL

Flip charts attached to an easel provide large, bold, and colorful images. The material can be prepared in advance or created on the spot. Most importantly, the speaker is not obscured by a darkened room or by an overhead projector that creates barriers.

BLACKBOARD

A blackboard, unlike an easel, allows room for a great quantity of material and enables the audience to think about everything that has been written down. As with any visual support, planning and clarity (in this case legible handwriting) will convey a professional image.

Room Setup

In setting up a room, try to maintain a direct and unobstructed view of every prospective member of the audience. For small groups, the room can be set up in classroom style with rows of chairs or tables. A U shape creates a sense of equality and provides no barriers between the speaker and each member of the audience.

Generally, speakers stand in the front center of a room with a lectern or table for notes. If an overhead projector is being used, the machine will be between some of the audience and the speaker, and the speaker will stand in between the audience and screen. In that case, project the image on a screen that is higher than your head. To prevent a distorted image, use a screen with a "keystone eliminator," a device that enables the top of the screen to tip forward. Another way to maintain a clear line of sight is to put the screen in the corner of the room. This is not always easy to do because screens are often permanently installed in the center of the room.

Audience and Speaker

By maintaining a clear line of slight with the audience, you can avoid the physical obstructions that create disinterest. If you use a pointer, you will be able to stand back far enough so that the audience can see you and the screen at the same time. When not referring to the screen, put the pointer down because it is insidious—it demands to be played with. If you speak directly in back of the overhead projector, using a pencil as a pointer that shows up on the screen, you can stay close to the lectern. However, move around enough so that the arm of the

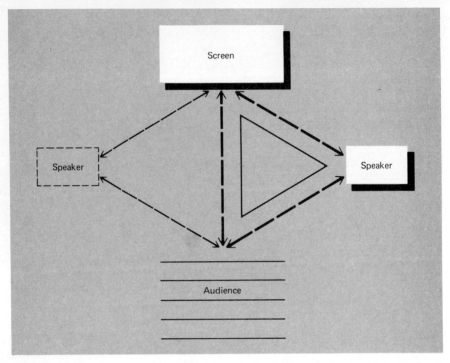

Figure 14-5   Screen placement.

projector does not break the line of sight between you and any member of the audience.

When used well, visual aids improve a presentation. Do not let them dominate. If the electricity fails, you should still be able to communicate. After all, speaking is telling and not showing.

Exercises

1   Design a visual aid containing only words. Write out the material first and revise it for clarity and conciseness. Transfer the words onto a sheet of paper that will fit into a cardboard frame used for overhead tansparencies. Experiment by printing, typing, or using press-apply letters. When you are satisfied with the contents and design of the material, go to a graphic arts department that makes transparencies. Have the transparency made, or make it yourself (a duplicated copy is usually necessary because the transparency maker picks up the carbon from the copy). Place the transparency in a cardboard frame.

2   Design a visual aid that illustrates an important idea. You can use a line or bar graph, a pie chart, a flowchart, or other graphic representations of data. Make a transparency and evaluate it for clarity. Does it show what you intended?

3   With the same material used for the transparency, draw an easel chart. Evaluate the transparency and the easel chart for ease of understanding. Determine which format is the most comfortable for you.

4   Find a room with an overhead projector. Put on one of the transparencies you have just made and sit in every part of the room. Where is the sight obstructed? How can you enable the entire audience to see everything at all times?

5   Prepare a brief presentation that would be improved by visual aids. Prepare the visuals, and give the presentation in front of an audience or video recorder. Evaluate the presentation for clarity and smoothness.

PART 4

Specific Tasks of Speaking

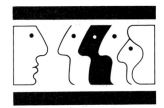

Chapter 15

Group Presentations

Planning

Working in groups differs from working individually, especially in oral presentations. A good editor can join parts of a written document into a coherent whole to give the product one voice. A group presentation consists of many voices, and the group must make these voices harmonize.

After determining the topic, audience, and purpose of the presentation, the group should examine its own capabilities. One person should be selected as group leader who will schedule meetings and oversee all problems of coordination. Determining who leads and who follows is a difficult task. In fact, some groups remain leaderless, or at least without a dominating force. Yet, at least for the sake of coordination someone in the group must assume nominal leadership. In situations where strong leadership can produce clear recommendations for action, leaders and followers will emerge so that the group can perform its job efficiently. The style of leadership within a group will vary according to the individuals and to the group's purpose. According to one account[1] of leadership styles:

There are many ways to Rome, and many ways to lead. One can command, persuade, suggest, or psychologically manipulate. Broadly speaking, how-

[1]Stanley E. Jones, Dean C. Barnlund, and Franklyn S. Haiman, *The Dynamics of Discussion* (New York: Harper & Row, 1980), p. 227.

165

ever, there are two main styles—autocratic and democratic—and most others are subtle variations of the two.

For the purpose of giving a presentation, the group should decide two issues of leadership—who will make the physical arrangements for the presentation and who will act as moderator. The group then should decide who will give the various parts of the presentation—introduction, subtopics, conclusion.

At the first meeting, the group should agree on format—length of individual presentations, consistent style of visual aids, methods of transition from one speaker to the next, and strategy for answering questions. The length of individual presentations should be about equal or appropriate to the importance of the subject. Visual aids should be consistent in format as well as content. If one person uses a bar graph to show comparisons, another should not use a line graph to show the same kinds of data. Likewise, for the sake of the overall consistency of a well-planned presentation, overhead transparencies, 35-mm slides, and easel charts should not be mixed without a good reason.

Transitions should be smooth. If a moderator does not provide transitions and introductions to each speaker, then the speaker must present a coordinated summary and transition: "I have covered the Metals Division, and now George Johnson, Vice President of Chemicals, will review new research in his area." Transitions do not have to be long or mechanical, but they should be well-planned.

If there is no official moderator, the last speaker can direct questions to appropriate group members. The group should decide beforehand who is best-qualified to answer questions not covered in the presentation. The audience will appreciate this kind of planning, and the group will not have to suffer the confusion of deciding on the spot who should answer.

Rehearsal

After the planning meetings, rehearsals begin. As in any speech, individuals should present all the material they have prepared, including at least a rough version of the visual aids. Do not leave gaps for material that is not ready. Gaps make it impossible to time and evaluate the first rehearsal, turning it into a useless exercise. Videotaping a rehearsal is always helpful, but in group presentations the audience is built-in. Each participant should comment on the organization, content, and style of all other speakers. With critical self-evaluation, the group can establish consistency of format, evaluate visual aids, and adjust content, deleting the irrelevant and adding new facts where necessary. Intensive criticism in the first rehearsal will make the job of revision easier because the group will become an audience looking for consistency.

Subsequent rehearsals will enable the group to polish individual presentations, become thoroughly familiar with visual aids, develop smooth transitions, and time the presentation exactly. If the presentation requires several visual aids, group members can help each other by managing the equipment. Anything the group can do to create a smooth presentation will be welcomed by an audience. Planning and professionalism are always impressive.

Rehearse as many time as needed to appear smooth but spontaneous. After each rehearsal, analyze the performance, using videotape if available. Evaluate changes, and do not be afraid to reintroduce something that appeared in earlier rehearsals. When nothing more can be gained from rehearsing and the group is comfortable with its material and format, then it is time for the presentation. Before your presentation, review the following checklist to see if preparation is complete.

CHECKLIST FOR GIVING GROUP PRESENTATIONS

I. Planning
  A. Establish Topic
  B. Determine Scope of Topic
    1. Type of material to be covered
    2. Amount of material to be covered
  C. Establish Purpose
    1. Information
    2. Persuasion
  D. Determine Audience
    1. Internal
      a. superiors
      b. subordinates
      c. peers
    2. External
      a. independent clients
      b. government agencies
      c. community groups
  E. Assign Participants
    1. Experts with thorough knowledge of subject
    2. Effective speakers
  F. Assign Tasks
    1. Group leader
    2. Introduction
    3. Major subtopics
    4. Conclusion

II. Preparation
  A. Independent Research
    1. Gather facts
    2. Assemble statistical support

    B. Group Meetings
        1. Become familiar with all aspects of topic
        2. Agree on format
            a. length of individual presentations
            b. consistent style of visual aids
            c. methods of transition from one speaker to next
            d. strategy for answering questions

III. Rehearsals
    A. First Rehearsal
        1. Present all material
        2. Time presentation
        3. Establish consistency of format and presentation style
        4. Adjust content
            a. analyze logic
            b. delete or add where necessary
    B. Other Rehearsals
        1. Polish individual presentation style
        2. Become thoroughly familiar with visual aids
        3. Time presentation precisely

Presentation

As in any presentation, examine the room well in advance, and hold rehearsals there if you can. Before the presentation begins, operate all microphones, projectors, and recording systems. Bring backup bulbs, extension cords, and cables. Likewise, bring your own manuscript and slides, trusting no one to deliver them for you! Always expect all equipment to fail and be prepared to give the presentation with words alone.

    If the group has any control over the schedule, the presentation should start on time (with only a few minutes grace), and it should end on time, leaving time for questions. A well-planned, well-rehearsed, and well-executed presentation is a persuasive form of communication.

Panel Discussions

Panel discussions mix the individual presentation with the group presentation. In preparing for a panel discussion, you should communicate with the leader or moderator to find out exactly what role you are to play. Duplication can be embarrassing to you and boring to the audience, and you can prevent this problem by planning.

Determine topic by agreeing to speak on a subcategory of the main issue. Then agree with the panel members on the format so that you all appear to be part of a group rather than individuals speaking randomly. Well in advance of the panel discussion, panel members should circulate outlines among themselves to make sure that the topic will be covered comprehensively. Time permitting, the final drafts of the panel presentations should also be circulated. After the presentation, the moderator will usually handle the questions-and-answer session, but if, as sometimes happens, no one is moderating, the group should appoint one of its own to direct questions to the right panel member and to manage the time of the discussion.

Some panel discussions do not require formal presentations, but the preparation should be just as serious. Once again, panel members should divide the topics among themselves, with individuals responsible for covering what they know best. Then, panel members should make up a list of general questions that they think the audience will ask of the whole group and a list of specific questions that an individual will want to answer. For example, in a discussion about the general plans of a company, the vice president of each division (operations, finance, research, etc.) should come prepared with relevant historical data and recommendations for further development. Even in this type of general panel discussion with no formal presentations, the presenters should keep in mind the specific goal of the discussion, and they should use the principles of effective speaking—unambiguous language and logic, clear enunciation and voice projection, efficient use of gestures.

Exercises

1   In the next group presentation you give, keep a log of the process from formation of the group to final presentation. After each meeting and rehearsal, analyze the effectiveness of the group. What problems occurred and how did you solve them?

2   In a group rehearsal, concentrate on transitions. Plan or write out the summary of a section with the introduction to the next speaker. As a group, decide on the content of the conclusion since the final words should bring together the points made by every speaker.

3   Rehearse the question-and-answer session that would normally follow the presentation. Determine who will be responsible for answering specific questions.

4   Prepare two conclusions to a presentation. Use the second one to finish the question-and-answer session. Do the two conclusions contain the same information?

5   Select a general topic for a panel discussion (a business plan, nuclear disarmament, retooling of industry) and divide the general topic into sub-categories. Assign each panel member the task of divising five questions with appropriate answers. Review all the questions to see if they cover the whole topic.

Chapter 16

Questions
and
Answers

Speakers who say they are more relaxed after the "formal" speech ends are fooling themselves. During the speech they are in complete control; during the questioning they may have to fight to maintain control. Since answering questions is a formal part of the speaking process, plan the process in the following way: write down five questions you *know* you will be asked; write down five questions you think you *may* be asked; write down the answers to all ten questions.

Questions are needed after most speeches. If members of the audience have been listening, they will want to respond, sometimes during the speech. Most often it is unwise to announce that the audience can interrupt with questions because too many interruptions will destroy the continuity of the speech. An occasional interruption will not hurt, however, especially if cutting someone off might antagonize. Nevertheless, the appropriate time for questions is after the speech. If you or your host make that announcement, the audience will usually not be rude and interrupt.

Guidelines for Answering Questions

ANTICIPATE QUESTIONS

The question-and-answer period should be as well-planned as the speech itself. As you prepare and rehearse your speech, try to respond to the audience's need to know, anticipating the questions you might be asked. What have you said that is controversial or questionable? What points are so complex that further explanation will always be helpful? What have you deliberately left out that you think is irrelevant but the audience might not? With these guidelines, write down a list of ten questions you think you will be asked and make some brief notes for the answers, including pertinent facts. You cannot be a prophet and anticipate all the questions. Half of what you write down will not be asked, and someone will always surprise you with an unanticipated question, usually simple in nature and not always relevant: "I know you are a scientist; what is your view on abortion?"

Whatever the questions, you should be prepared with additional data not covered in your speech but supportive of your main ideas. This additional information is like an appendix. With it you can tell the audience as much or as little as you like.

UNDERSTAND THE QUESTION

The speaker must understand the question and must make sure the audience understands it. If the question seems to be ambiguous, paraphrase it and ask the questioner to agree to your interpretation or clarify the question. If you are certain someone in the audience has not heard the question, repeat it. Invariably, the person with the softest voice will sit in the front of the room and whisper the question. You owe it to the audience to let them in on the secret. Do not repeat all questions, however; you will waste time and sound monotonous.

PLAN THE ANSWER

If you have anticipated most of the questions, you can answer from a brief written outline. If you are not completely prepared for the question, make some notes or a mental outline as the questioner speaks. Start with the conclusion: *yes, no, by means of,* or *because.* Then fill in the details in a logical sequence, referring to your speech or to additional data you have at hand. Answer in concise, but not clipped, statements; amplify your answer with examples, without giving another speech. You may be so well-prepared that you spend too long on the answer. Give the audience a chance to respond.

DO NOT DIGRESS

If you are asked a simple question, do not use too many examples or personal anecdotes. You can give a complete answer in about one minute; an expanded answer should take no more than three minutes. Who will be counting the minutes? If you do not, the audience will.

BE HONEST

Sooner or later you will be asked a question you cannot answer. Do not bluff or attempt an answer and fail. If you know you cannot answer, say, perhaps with a valid excuse: "I'm sorry I don't know the answer to your question. I'm in the accounting department. I can tell you what the costs are but not how the item is made." You also can offer to find out the answer: "I don't have that information, but I know where to find it. Give me your name after we finish, and I'll send you the answer."

If you are asked uncomfortable questions, be honest by giving complete answers. Do not leave out information that may not support your case, but use all the facts you have that will show that your solution is better. The audience will appreciate your acknowledging the opposition. They also will quickly note if you leave out an important point or if you otherwise obfuscate. If you lost money last year, say so, and then remind the audience that you showed an increase of 5 to 10 percent in the past five years.

REINTERPRET LOADED QUESTIONS

Only in unusual circumstances will a questioner launch a direct attack. More likely the challenge will come in the form of innuendo or sarcasm. Nevertheless, you might hear: "You don't know what you are talking about. You say you help people, but how come my brother-in-law can't get a loan?" To respond to this kind of challenge, first reestablish credibility and try to remove personalities: "I am branch manager, but I do not know your brother-in-law." Then generalize, showing the similarities to other situations or organizations: "Your question seems to concern not only our bank's policy but the way all banks approach lending."

CONTROL INTERCHANGES

If a hostile questioner persists, you can cut him off by saying: "Let's discuss personal problems after the speech and give someone else a chance." If he still will not stop, he officially becomes a heckler. Appeal to the audience and try to continue: "I think we all agree that these questions are not pertinent. Is there someone else who has a relevant question?" Speakers have a responsibility not to let any member of the audience dominate the questions. If someone asks too many questions, go out of your way to call on another questioner. If a question is beginning to turn into a speech, you have a right to interrupt and ask speakers to rephrase their thoughts into a brief question. Remember that if you have been persuasive, the audience will be on your side and show disapproval of a heckler. In turn, you owe it to the audience to control the question-and-answer period.

Some questioners, though well-intended, will digress from your stated subject. When responding to digressive questions, refer to your speech, keeping the audience on your track and stimulating them to ask pertinent questions. You can control a question-and-answer session without being aggressive or rude if you keep the goal of the presentation in your own mind and in the minds of the audience.

USE THE LAST QUESTION TO SUMMARIZE

When you know there will be time for one more question, listen carefully and try to relate the answer to the general context of your speech. Answer the question concisely, and then show how the specific question relates to the entire speech: "Yes, we have increased the size and number of loans in your area, a direct result of the way our bank policy is made—the topic of my speech." Then summarize and restate very briefly the major points of the speech, concluding with the message you wish to communicate. Leave your audience with the impression that you were organized and in control from your first word to your last.

Asking Questions

Communication can be improved if questions are clear. Questioners often garble their thoughts, digress, or start to give speeches of their own. Some are afraid to ask in a loud voice so that at least half of the audience is not a part of the supposed communication.

Those who ask questions can prevent embarrassment by making very brief notes before they speak. It does not take much time to write out a simple question or even to make a brief outline of a two- or three-part question. Writing down or verbalizing questions in your mind will help you eliminate ambiguity and force the speaker to give a direct answer. Speak with strength and project your voice so that everyone can hear you. If the audience is large or the acoustics are bad, stand up. When you have finished, do not repeat or rephrase the question. Place the burden of clarification on the speaker.

Exercises

1   Practice asking questions at the next presentation you attend. Find out all you can about the speaker and topic before you go so that you will be prepared to understand the presentation. During the speech, formulate questions and write them down. If your questions have not been answered, choose the most important one and write down a word or phrase that will allow you to ask an intelligent question. Do not write out the question, but go over it in your own mind to make it simple to ask and to be understood.

2   For the next presentation you give, prepare a list of questions you think you will be asked. If the possible questions relate to the specific part of your presentation, make notes that will allow you to remind yourself and the questioner about what you have said. If the questions will refer to material not specifically covered in the presentation, plan an answer by having necessary facts at hand and by writing out a brief concluding point.

3   With a group of friends, try to respond to hostile or semihostile questions. Try to diffuse a personal attack by generalizing the question.

4   Prepare a second conclusion to your presentation to be used as the answer to the final question. This second conclusion should summarize the main points of the presentation and the anticipated questions.

Chapter 17

Meetings

The Formal Meeting

The meeting is the opium of bureaucracy. It puts most participants to sleep and lulls others into believing that something is being accomplished. Yet, if properly run, meetings can be a forum for an exchange of ideas leading to action.

Two people can hold an informal meeting and, if they have the authority, accomplish as much as an entire board. Large groups often accomplish little if the meeting is not planned with a structure and a goal. The word *meeting* in this chapter means a formal, scheduled gathering that requires preparation.

Preparation

Running a meeting is a form of public speaking; therefore, careful preparation for meetings is as important as it is for speeches. The outline for the meeting is the agenda. No general laws govern agendas, but logic, precedent, and specific procedures established by individual organizations create a sequence of topics. After the call to order and approval of the minutes, the agenda customarily includes a president's or chairman's report, treasurer's report, old business, and new business. Another item, committee reports, might be placed before new business, especially if committees are directed to report regularly. If you are running a meeting, contact all presenters to discuss the nature and length of the reports. Insist on preliminary copies of reports, motions, or resolutions. An extraordinary amount of time can be saved if a motion can be checked for validity, clarity, and consistency before it is presented for interpretation. If the presenter agrees to sensible changes before parliamentary debate results in tedious amendments, participants will have more time to discuss the validity of the proposed action.

After establishing the general agenda, arrange subtopics. Related topics should appear consecutively so that discussion of one issue leads naturally into the next. For example, the topic of general financial issues can be followed by a specific proposal for new research. Limiting the number of subtopics will help prevent meetings that fail because too much is planned.

It is the leader's responsibility to allot time for reports and discussion. The amount of time scheduled depends on the importance or controversiality of the topic and on the wordiness of the presenters. Bend a little to personalities, while adhering to a time limit.

After the sequence and timing are planned, distribute the agenda at least three days in advance of the meeting. The agenda should be accompanied by a meeting notice, stating time and place, and by any supplementary material that will help participants prepare. If the leader sets the standard for preparation, the participants will know they cannot "do their homework" in the hall.

Running a Meeting

To run meetings effectively, establish a record of punctuality, starting and finishing on time. If gathering a quorum proves difficult, contact attendees beforehand and ask them to show up on time. After a few meetings the message will become clear. Then it is your responsibility to see that meetings finish punctually. Individuals value their time and are understandably upset when meetings wander.

As a convenience, provide extra copies of previously disseminated material. In meetings and speeches, printed material should not distract the audience but should provide information that needs no explanation. It is always a waste of time to read handouts to literate people.

Introduce all topics listed on the agenda, briefly reviewing background, current situation, and possible action, if such a statement is not prejudicial. Also, make transitions between topics, summarizing completed action and showing relationships, if any, to succeeding items. Control but do not dominate the discussion. Apply parliamentary procedure judiciously, remembering that procedures are not laws and that some flexibility is efficient. Step in to summarize debate when points are being repeated or digressions occur. Do not take arbitrary action to limit debate but suggest appropriate procedures—time limits, tabling, calling the question.

If a moderator is too domineering, the meeting becomes a list of announcements or a personal forum. Such a leader diminishes the sense of democracy implied by a meeting and destroys the motivation to offer creative solutions. A weak moderator is equally ineffective. Without an authoritative and well-prepared leader, a meeting can degenerate into digression or inaction and can be dominated by those who are trying to seize authority. An authoritative moderator combines formal speaking techniques with the art of informal interchange, giving clear introductions, summaries, and conclusions and practicing the techniques of successful delivery—good posture, diction, and voice projection. The moderator also should be capable of friendly, although succinct, interchange with colleagues. The most successful leader of a meeting is one who interprets and guides, but rules when necessary.

Unless you wish to turn the meeting into a forum for your own views, questions and answers are the most common form of communication. As any good speaker would do, paraphrase, interpret, or repeat the question so that everyone has heard and understood. Do not try to answer all questions; instead call on experts who have the ability to give clear answers.

The final step in running a meeting effectively is summarizing. No matter how late the hour and even if people are walking out, take one or two minutes (no more) to summarize the significant results, remind the group of any action to be taken, and announce the next meeting. You should have the last word—not your own opinion but a summary of the assembly's wishes.

Participating in a Meeting

Regardless of the moderator's preparation, the success of a meeting depends on the participants. When you are called to a meeting, read all supporting material, including minutes of the previous meeting, well in advance. Prepare and rehearse individal reports or presentations. Try not to read reports because meetings, more than speeches, require the spontaneity of personal communication among the participants.

Understand basic parliamentary procedure. A motion results in action and is introduced by the words, "I move." A resolution is a formal demonstration of support or disapproval requiring no action and is introduced by "I resolve" or "Be it resolved." A point of information is a request for clarification related to the specific business being discussed; a point of order is a challenge to a procedure. The terms "point of order" and "point of information" are often confused. When used too often, they turn a meeting into a procedural tangle that often characterizes legislative proceedings of governments. The effective paticipant of a meeting should know when and how to use parliamentary procedure.[1]

---

[1] See Henry M. Robert, *Robert's Rules of Order: Newly Revised* (Glenview, IL: Scott, Foresman, 1981).

Guidelines for Participating in Meetings

Knowing parliamentary procedure is part of the necessary preparation for meetings; it is part of the homework that includes knowing the agenda and reviewing any documents pertinent to the discussions. For the meeting itself, remember these guidelines:

Be prompt: Promptness is a sign of reliability.

Be alert: For the sake of the meeting and yourself, pay attention at all times, and do not ask a question that has already been asked.

Be brief: In meetings, speechmakers are tedious. Limit comments or questions to a single issue.

Be objective: Put emotion aside unless it is backed by logic.

Be silent: Do not repeat what others have said. Either keep quiet or simply note agreement with another speaker.

When making a statement or asking a question, take the time to write a brief outline before opening your mouth. In the heat of discussion and with the pressure to be concise, it is easy to forget a main point unless you write it down. Make your own notes on important issues, especially those that concern you. Minutes are interpretations and condensations. If you need to question the interpretation, your own notes will help you remember what took place.

Speak up in a meeting. Remember to project your voice and use clear diction. In a large group, stand up and speak to everyone in the room, establishing good eye contact. When supported by fact and logic, a strong voice commands respect.

Finally, be courteous. Do not read or hold private conversations. Avoid personal attack because most meetings concern issues and not personalities. You can amplify your own personal strengths by remembering that a meeting is a form of communication, requiring the skills of logic, organization, and oratory.

Exercises

1 Type out a meeting agenda. List standard items established by convention or bylaw and specific issues to be discussed. Make sure items listed are grammatically consistent.

2 Outline a committee report on recent activity. At the end of the outline, write a specific motion to be considered by the group.

3 In the next meeting you attend, determine what was effective and what failed. Look especially for preparation, internal summaries, and ability to move the meeting forward. How did the moderator handle difficult problems or personalities?

4 In the next meeting you chair, concentrate on internal summaries and transitions from one point on the agenda to the next. Make notes as the meeting progresses so that you can also prepare a cogent summary of the entire meeting.

Chapter 18

Interviewing

Few people think of an interview as a form of public speaking. Yet the principles of effective communication apply in a situation where careers are at stake. An interview is a two-way communication. It need not be a stressful experience in which the person with power dominates. With research, planning, and self-assurance the person being interviewed can communicate as an equal with an interviewer.

The purpose of interviews is to gain specific information; therefore, the type of information needed determines the type of interview. Job interviews represent the most common type; other important purposes for interviews include the college interview, evaluation interview, information interview, and the exit interview. Whether you are the interviewer or the person being interviewed, all types require effective communication skills: planning, writing, speaking, and listening.

Job Interview

The job interview becomes a process of discovery. Each party explores the potential of the other. The interviewer should be able to judge how the candidate will fit the needs of the organization, and the interviewee should be able to assess the ability to do the job while fulfilling personal needs for satisfaction and advancement. The job interview is crucial for determining the future.

THE CANDIDATE

Successful job interviews require careful preparation. Since the purpose of the interview is to judge potential, the effective interviewer tries to bring out the good qualities of an individual, knowing that the candidate may be apprehensive. The candidate can remove some of the stress by adequate preparation.

Too many people go into interviews playing a role and trying to impress. Be yourself. Stress ability and potential in job interviews with self-assurance but not with arrogance. Interviewers want to discover your true personality so that they can judge your potential for efficient and creative work.

PREPARATION

Research.   When you confront the public (one or more persons), preparation strengthens credibility and self-assurance. For a job interview, adequate preparation can eliminate elementary questions and shows that you have taken the initiative to learn about the institution. A good place to begin is in a public or college library. Business libraries will have annual reports of the large companies as well as important reference tools like Dun and Bradstreet's *Million Dollar Directory* for addresses and Moody's *Manuals* for financial information. Learn the names of chief officers, locations of facilities, product or type of business, gross revenue, and recent achievements or problems. If the company is local and small, look for information in a trade publication or find someone with personal knowledge of the organization. Make enough notes so that you will remember details during the interview. Do not show off by reciting the information the interviewer knows. Instead, use one or two facts as part of a statement or question: "With gross revenues of about $770 million, do you intend to increase spending on research?"

Qualifications. The next step in the preparation is to establish your usefulness to the company and especially to the job being offered. Honestly assess your experience, education, qualifications, and potential. Then evaluate the way the company operates to see if *it* is qualified to meet your needs. For example, some firms are too big and demanding for those who do not want a sixteen hour a day, pressure-filled job. Look carefully at your résumé to see where you can prove to yourself and your interviewer that you are qualified. Emphasize personal experience and potential.

Appearance.   Appearance helps create a first impression; how you look signifies how you want to look. Clean clothes, coordinated colors, and combed hair are all important signs of self-assurance and forethought. In an interview, flashy or casual clothes are like wordiness in writing; they call attention to the form and not to the substance. Men should wear suits and ties to acknowledge the formal nature of the interview. Suits are also appropriate for women, but so are tailored dresses. Apparel for subsequent interviews can change after the candidate assesses the standards or flexibility of the organization. Dress in a way that exhibits self-confidence and comfort. Ask yourself how you want to look and what you think the interviewer would like to see and then create an appearance that represents your true personality.

Effective speaking. If you appear self-confident, you should sound that way, too, without being overly aggressive. An interview is a public appearance, so you must concentrate on voice projection and posture. Although the interview is a conversation, do not lapse into slang and sloppy pronunciation, but do not be pretentious either by trying to use big words to show how much you know. Speak in a normal tone, and breathe properly so that you do not sound nervous or weak. Do not play a role in an interview (being deliberately soft-spoken or aggressive) because under pressure you will either forget the role or, worse, change your personality to the role you have assumed.

Names. When you introduce yourself, speak clearly and listen carefully. Learn the names of the interviewers and use those names during and especially at the end of the interview. If you have trouble remembering names, look for a diploma or name plate and write down the name unobtrusively. Even if you cannot remember all the names, do the best you can. Your efforts will be appreciated.

Answering questions. After the introduction and polite chatting, the interview will become a series of questions and answers. Prepare for this beforehand by writing down the question you think you will be asked and making some notes about the answers you want to give. Remember that the interviewer wants to find a person who will do the job well now and in the future. General job interview questions include:

1 What have you done?

2 What can you do?

3 What are your compensation requirements?

4 What are your strengths?

5 What are your weaknesses?

While you are being asked a specific question, begin to plan the answer. First, make sure you understand the question, and if you do not, ask the interviewer to repeat it. Then think about the conclusion—the simple answer. Support the conclusion with personal experience or information drawn from the résumé. Since the résumé is an outline of the interview, be sure to bring two copies, one for you and one for the interviewer if necessary. Be especially careful to answer only what is asked. People who talk too much in interviews appear disorganized and try the patience of the interviewer.

Start with a simple answer, use examples or data as support, and conclude with a very brief summary: "So I would say that my experience as assistant manager qualifies me for this job." As you answer, watch for signs of impatience from the interviewer, but do not leave out an important part of your answer just because someone frowns. Do not be intimidated; use your answer to show strength, and if you do not know the answer, say so.

Asking questions.   Asking questions is as important as answering them. Prepare by writing down what you want to ask and what has not been answered in your research. Ask questions, if appropriate, during the interview or save them until the end. When asking a question, you switch roles and take control of the conversation. Do not press too hard by asking irrelevant questions or for confidential information. When the question is answered, stop talking and allow the roles to reverse again.

Trouble.   Be prepared for trouble. As one story goes, an interviewer asks the candidate to open a window that has been locked or nailed shut. The "true" personality of the candidate is supposed to come through in the struggle to do the impossible. This is a game. The interviewer has the responsibility to avoid trickery, and the candidate has a responsibility to exhibit self-respect. In such a situation, if the window will not open, ask for help.

More often, trouble comes in the form of a personality clash or in incomplete or incorrect answers. Even if interviewer and candidate do not like each other, the candidate should try to remain congenial and objective, making sure that the important questions are answered. If you say the wrong thing, do not hesitate to correct yourself, even later in the interview. Also, do not be afraid to start an answer over if you need to clarify. Interviews are stressful, but in most cases the interviewer wants the candidate to demonstrate strength, not weakness.

Conclusion.   You can show strength and understanding by your own summary and conclusion to the interview. Agree on further action and thank the interviewer by name. A firm handshake and a polite exit will close the interview and may open the way to a job.

Follow-up.   Follow-up is essential and should be immediate. Within twenty-four hours mail a letter of thanks, briefly reviewing your appropriateness for the job. You may also wish to include a writing sample or a description of how you would complete a task mentioned in the interview. For example, if part of the job is to begin a new project, type out a description and schedule of how you would like to see things done. Creativity and initiative always help in getting a job.

If you were told you would receive a response on a given date and you have not heard anything, wait one or two more days and then write a letter politely reminding the interviewer of the need for a decision. Use the telephone only if something new or important has occurred or if other offers or your present position require a decision. Be prepared to keep looking for jobs until the day you sit down at your new desk. Even then, update your résumé regularly.

College Interview

The college interview can be intimidating if the candidate believes the purpose is to find reasons for turning down an application. The opposite is true: colleges want to explore a candidate's potential based on prior achievements, poise, and enthusiasm for learning. In many college interviews, the questions will usually fall into three categories:

1 Tell me about yourself.

2 Why do you want to come here?

3 What plans do you have for the future?

Some interviewers might ask the candidate to ask questions about the school. By reading the college catalog or by talking to a student or alumnus, you will eliminate obvious questions, saving time for a more perceptive question that shows forethought.

Your personality should come through in an interview. Dress comfortably with proper attention to style of clothing. As in any form of communication, consider your audience and anticipate their standards while maintaining your own standards for good taste.

Speak up! Even though you may be nervous, direct answers will demonstrate self-confidence. Do not be afraid of making mistakes; if you do not like what you have said, start over or correct yourself. Remember that a college interview is a conversation with a double purpose. The college wants to find out if you are a strong candidate for admission, and you want to decide whether you want to be accepted by that particular school. When the meeting is over, thank the interviewer, and as soon as you can, write a note to show your continued interest.

Evaluation Interview

Evaluation interviews provide an opportunity to analyze projects or performance. For example, a research director might call in a department head every month to discuss the current status of a project. For this type of interview, both participants need to have a clear understanding of the project and the responsibilities for completing it. Facts are essential: personnel involved, equipment, costs, schedules. The purpose of this type of interview is to communicate information.

Performance evaluation interviews require guidelines. If the job description is clear, and if a job evaluation form is available to supervisor and employee, the evaluation interview can be constructive and not stressful. In many organizations, the employee fills out a self-evaluation form before the interview. The interview then has a structure that should cover the major elements of job performance. To prepare for the interview, the employee should anticipate constructive criticism and show an understanding of the job's needs. Preparation for this interview will demonstrate responsibility. Control excess emotions in a personnel interview. Being defensive or aggressive often detracts from the goal of objective evaluation.

The exit interview is another form of evaluation. Some people may see this exercise as a way to criticize the organization—to say what they always wanted to but could not because they needed to keep working. Exit interviews are not a place to vent emotions, especially behind someone's back. Make a list of the positive and the negative sides of your organization. If you have had any loyalty to the organization, your constructive criticisms may improve what you think is a bad situation. Since the exit interview becomes part of the company records, do not make statements you will regret, even though you are leaving.

Information Interview

Information interviews place the responsibility on the interviewer. In surveys, the interviewer must ask questions that can be understood and answered easily. Decide what you want to find out and conduct an interview that will give you specific answers. Begin with the general and move to the specific, or start with questions of fact and end with opinions. Research and pretesting will help you achieve the goal of this type of information interview.

Newspaper and magazine interviews require skill in uncovering the facts. Organize questions *before* the interview. You need to know *who?, what?, when?, where?,* and *why?,* but you should ask these questions in specific terms: "Why have you decided to sell the food division?" Before any interview, find out as much as you can about your subject so that you do not waste time on the obvious.

Establishing your own credibility will instill confidence that the interviewee's words will not be garbled.

Responsibilities of the Interviewer

An interview is a two-way process requiring communication skills for all participants. The interviewee should try to anticipate the questions asked, and the interviewer should structure the interview in order to discover as much as possible during a brief encounter. In a job interview, preparation for the interviewer includes a thorough knowledge of the position, supported by an accurate and clearly written job description. The interviewer also should review the candidate's résumé carefully and try to discuss all the major items during the interview.

The structure of the interview should include an explanation of the job, specific preplanned questions, answers about job benefits, working conditions, promotions, etc. The interviewer should explore the candidate's strengths, managerial potential, and outside interests. A good interviewer will uncover weaknesses such as dishonesty (gaps or exaggerations in the résumé), lack of preparation, vagueness, digression, and general lack of enthusiasm or competence for the job. On the last issue, an interviewer should note that a candidate who might lack competence for one job might be the right person for another job.

Before the interview, establish criteria for judgment in order to make a fair evaluation. These criteria include education, experience, and demonstrated achievement. Personal attributes include verbal skills, motivation, creativity, and the ability to get along with others and to accept criticism.

In order to make accurate judgments, the interviewer has the responsibility to listen as well as to talk. The purpose of an interview is, after all, to find the right person for the job, and that purpose can be accomplished by clearly communicating needs and allowing the candidate to respond to those needs.

At the end of the interview, restate the job's responsibilities and set up a schedule for notification. When you have made a decision, respond personally to the candidate either by telephone or letter. A personal response signifies communication between human beings.

Exercises

1   To prepare for a college interview, make a personal profile of your experience, strengths, and goals. Add to the list significant events in your life, especially ones that demonstrate strong character and success. Make a list of questions you would like to be asked about yourself.

2   Choose three college catalogs and prepare a list of questions you would like to ask an interviewer. Do not ask for information already contained in the catalog.

3   For a job interview, review your résumé, and make a list of questions you think you will be asked. Be sure to notice time lapses, career changes, significant work experience, and important personal traits.

4   Choose three organizations where you would want to work, and find out as much as you can about them in their annual reports or other published profiles. Make a list of questions you would like to ask in an interview.

5   Exchange résumés with a friend, and practice interviewing. When you play the role of the interviewer, review the résumé carefully, and make a list of questions that pertain to each section of the résumé. Add questions that the résumé does not cover, and plan how to close the interview. Reverse the roles and ask the same questions.

APPENDIX 1

Glossary of Style and Usage

The terms in this glossary describe common problems that hinder clear writing and speaking. The list is by no means exhaustive; standard grammar books will be useful supplements to the library of anyone who writes or makes oral presentations. Knowing the terms in the glossary will help you revise your own work or edit the work of others. If you can identify the problem, especially a problem that keeps showing up, you will know what you have to correct in order to be clear.

Grammar

Agreement (agr).   When subject and verb or antecedent and pronoun are not in the same number (singular with singular, plural with plural), agreement errors occur. Another type of agreement error, shift in number, occurs when the point of view changes from the third person to the second person.

SUBJECT AND VERB

Error		Correction
SINGULAR SUBJECT + PLURAL VERB	A complete set of documents *are* enclosed.	A complete set of documents *is* enclosed.
PLURAL SUBJECT + SINGULAR VERB	The profits from the sale *was* large.	The profits from the sale *were* large.
COMPOUND PLURAL SUBJECT + SINGULAR VERB	The president and the general manager *has* announced a new benefits program.	The president and the general manager *have* announced a new benefits program.

ANTECEDENT AND PRONOUN

Error		Correction
SINGULAR ANTECEDENT + PLURAL PRONOUN	Each member is required to keep *their* own time sheets.	Each member of the firm is required to keep his or her own time sheet.

SHIFT IN NUMBER

Error		Correction
THIRD PERSON TO SECOND PERSON	Good writers do not shift *your* point of view.	Good writers do not shift *their* point of view.

Case.   A common mistake is to use the nominative ("I") instead of the objective case ("me") after a preposition. Also, the intensive or reflexive pronoun *myself* is often used instead of the objective.

Error	Correction
Would you like to go to lunch with Dave and *I*?	Would you like to go to lunch with Dave and *me*?
Please return the memo to my secretary or *myself*.	Please return the memo to my secretary or *me*.

Comma fault (cf).   Sentences with comma faults contain too many independent clauses (each with its own subject and verb) without proper punctuation. When joining independent clauses without a conjunction, do not use a comma. Use a semicolon or write two sentences. A semicolon is necessary when using an adverbial conjunction (*however, therefore, nevertheless,* etc.).

Error	Correction
The company closed four of its branches, they also reorganized the sales division.	The company closed four of its branches, *and* they also reorganized the sales division. (Or: "branches; they")
The president was hopeful, however sales were still down.	The president was hopeful; however, sales were still down.

Dangling modifier (dm).   A dangling modifier is a clause that is not related to the rest of the sentence because the subject cannot do what the verbal modifier describes.

Error	Correction
Having no contact with subordinates, *these notions* of worker incompetency will grow rather than diminish.	Having no contact with subordinates, *managers* will continue to believe that workers are incompetent.

Impersonal construction (imp).   This imp creates an ambiguous relationship between the pronoun *it* and the apparent antecedent. *It is often* said that the impersonal construction is overused.

Error	Correction
The supervisor asked Mr. Mason to rewrite the report. *It* was unclear if *he* would do *it*.	The supervisor asked Mr. Mason to rewrite the report. *Mason* was not sure whether he *would comply*. (Or: The *supervisor* was not sure whether *Mason* would comply.)

Misplaced modifier (mm).   Modifiers that are out of place confuse the reader. Put adverbs close to the words they modify. To avoid ambiguity or redundancy, do not split an infinitive or place an adverb between the helping verb and main verb. Break this traditional rule before distorting a sentence.

SPLIT INFINITIVE

1   Redundant—to *absolutely* refuse

2   Confusing—to *further* confuse (further is a verb as well as an adverb)

3   Awkward—to *properly, thoroughly, firmly,* and *sensitively* explain.

MODIFIER OUT OF PLACE

He left work early also. (He also left work early.)

SQUINTING MODIFIER
(AMBIGUOUS REFERENCE TO MORE THAN ONE CONSTRUCTION)

The institutions that we supported substantially improved their services. (*Substantially* could modify either verb.)

Mood.   Verbs convey meaning in three ways: the imperative mood, the indicative mood, and the subjunctive mood. Imperative verbs command, indicative verbs declare or describe, and subjunctive verbs suggest actions that have not occurred. Rumors of the demise of the subjunctive in English are truly exaggerated. Many remain: possibility, probability, hope, doubt, wish, and condition contrary to fact. Of these five, the two most common are wish and contradiction. Many words introducing the subjunctive are followed by *that.* (I doubt that . . . ; It is important that . . . ; I recommend that . . . .)

Error	Correction
I wish you *was* here.	I wish you *were* here.
It is important that he *attends.*	It is important that he *attend.*

Parallel structure.   When writers or speakers mix grammatical constructions, faulty parallelism results. Constructions that are not parallel usually appear in a series or in lists. Lists beginning with different grammatical forms are especially confusing because the entries do not have equal weight or importance.

Error	Correction
To read, to write, and keeping silent are difficult.	*Reading, writing,* and *keeping silent* are difficult.
I watched while I *wait.*	I watched while I *waited.*

The schedule follows:
    Transfer from airport.
    Checking into hotel.
    To shop.
    Everyone will return at nightfall.
	The schedule follows:
	    transfer from airport;
	    hotel check-in;
	    shopping tour;
	    return to hotel at nightfall.

Reference (ref).   Faulty pronoun reference confuses the reader. A pronoun refers to the noun immediately preceding it and cannot refer to an entire sentence or paragraph. A good way to clarify the relationship between antecedent and pronoun is to repeat the antecedent if it is too far away from the pronoun.

Error	Correction
The *meeting* was boring, *which* I knew would happen.	I *knew* the *meeting* would be boring.
Make love not war. *It* is better for you.	Make love not war; *love* is better for you.

Tense.   Ambiguity of time results when a writer mixes tenses within a sentence or paragraph. Rely on the present tense as often as possible, and use the past tense for completed actions. When discussing hypothetical cases, use the present tense as if the action were taking place today.

Error	Correction
The committee proposes new programs, but it *did* nothing to implement them.	The committee proposes new programs, but it *does* nothing to implement them.

Voice.   The active voice emphasizes action and shows clear relationships between the actor and the action taken. The passive voice is used to provide variation in sentence patterns and to remove personal involvement. The passive is not wrong, but overuse leads to ambiguity and wordiness.

Weak	Strong
Assignments *were prioritized* by the manager on a daily basis.	Every day the manager *assigned* a list of priorities.
A compromise *was agreed upon* by all participants.	All participants *agreed* to compromise.

Usage

Ambiguity (amb).   Sometimes a word or phrase can have more than one meaning. Unless such ambiguity is deliberate, you should clarify your meaning to the reader.

Ambiguous	Clear
The government reported that unemployment had *improved.*	The government reported that unemploy- had *decreased.*

Awkward (awk).   Sentences with words or phrases out of place are awkward and sound like a crow: (awk!). Put words, phrases, or clauses close to their antecedents.

Awkward	Clear
Too many variables are left untreated that have important impacts on projects.	Too many variables that effect profits are left untreated.

Cliché.   Sometimes perfectly good words become overused, losing specific meaning. People who use clichés cannot achieve a style of their own because their writing sounds like everybody else's. In order to achieve individuality, the careful writer will avoid clichés such as the following:

On a daily basis

A better bottom line

Water over the dam

On the right track

Take the ball and run with it

Diction (d).   The term *diction* can refer to enunciation or to word choice. The two main types of diction are formal and informal; problems of diction occur when the formal becomes pretentious with an overabundance of polysyllabic Latinate words and when the informal deteriorates to (you know) slang or colloquialism. Be consistent in the use of diction, and do not be afraid to use the simple and concrete instead of the pretentious and abstract. Achieving simplicity is difficult for those who *utilize* instead of *use* and cannot hear the difference.

Formal	Informal
intuition	gut feelings

Pretentious	Simple
Effecting an emulsion by intensive agitation is necessary for adequate product utilization.	Shake well before using.

Jargon.   In Old French, jargon meant *prattle of birds*. The word appeared in English about 1340, translated to human terms with a negative connotation: *unintelligible talk, hybrid speech.* According to Fowler's *Dictionary of American-English Usage* by Margaret Nicholson, there are three types of jargon:

"1) the sectional vocabulary of a science, art, class, sect, trade or profession, full of technical terms; 2) hybrid speech of different languages; 3) the use of long words, circumlocution, and other clumsiness."[1] Jargon is not necessarily "evil," but writers who rely on deadening language show contempt for their readers. Contempt does not lead to effective communication!

EXAMPLES OF JARGON

Words with limited meanings, used for a specific purpose:

The interface of two chemical elements results in a recombination.

Hybrid mixture of languages:

A priori, never makes any *ad hoc* assumptions about the *status quo* of our *lingua franca, ceteris paribus*.

Fashionable words, sometimes coinages, where specific meaning is not clear:

1 *Interface*—used in relation to computers; misused when referring to humans. The only time people can interface is when they kiss.

2 *Hire*—used as a noun instead of the common, *employee*. Instead of *new hire*, use *newly hired employee* or *new employee*.

3 *Trade-off*—vague because of several possible meanings: *compromise; giving up something for something better, worse, or equal; barter.*

4 *User-friendly*—a coinage relating to computers, in an attempt to humanize a machine.

5 *Time horizon, time frame*—coinages that yoke two dimensions in an illogical manner. Time horizon is a mixture of time and space, and time frame makes the best sense if the "guts" are taken out of a watch. Both words usually mean *schedule*.

Metaphor (met).   Metaphors are necessary for good writing because the use of figurative language explains things by *calling up mental pictures*. Consistent metaphors are useful; mixed metaphors are ludicrous.

1 A consistent, useful metaphor: "My cup runneth over."

2 A consistent, but trite metaphor: "You know it's raining to beat the band by the drumming on the roof."

---

[1]Margaret Nicholson, *A Dictionary of American-English Usage Based on Fowler's Modern English Usage* (New York: Signet, 1958).

3 Mixed Metaphors—"Dr. Max Rafferty said, 'When you take off this straightjacket, you introduce a lot of wild cards into the game on which we shall have to ride herd.' This is almost in a class with Frederick J. Grew's: 'We shall vigorously fly through the horns of this dilemma and plough our course to the stirring target of our goal until we sail into the harbor which beckons to us from its lofty pinnacle.' As the late great Jim McSheehy might have said, and did: 'The handwriting on the wall is as clear as a bell.' "—Quoted from Herb Caen's column in the San Francisco *Chronicle*.

Redundant (red). Redundancy is a form of repetition in which more than one word conveys a single concept.

1 Refer back (refer)

2 End result (result)

3 Consensus of opinion (consensus)

4 At this point in time (now)

5 First of all (first)

6 Completely finished (finished)

Repetition (rep). This term refers to the repetition of complete ideas or of individual words. Sometimes, repetition is an effective rhetorical device; most often, repetition causes wordiness:

REPETITION OF WORDS

Empirical investigations into the optimal financial structure of a *firm* and the use of the capital asset pricing model have *firmly* established their statistical validity for domestic firms.

REPETITION OF IDEAS

Investing successfully in the stock market requires research, surveillance, and luck. Good fortune helps. (Unless a pun is intended, the latter sentence is repetitive.)

Wrong word (ww). Many words sound alike, and their meanings are often confused. Other words are used incorrectly because they do not mean what we think they do.

1 Continual—recurring regularly, usually in rapid succession
Continuous—occurring without interruption

2 Fortuitous—occurring by chance
Fortunate—receiving some unexpected good

3 Cohort—one of ten divisions of a Roman legion
Colleague—an associate

Logic and Organization

The following terms refer to problems of organization and logic as opposed to syntax.

Logic (log). Faulty syllogisms, incomplete inductive arguments, circular reasoning, and other problems of logic weaken the organization of a paragraph or the overall organization of an extended argument. As the first step in analyzing logic, take the *how-and-why*? or *how much*? tests. Most defects of logic are caused by incomplete information.

Organization (org). Sometimes paragraphs or groups of paragraphs do not adhere to a logical sequence (chronological, categorical, spatial, etc.). To examine organization, put a letter or number next to each paragraph or sentence. Rearrange to achieve a logical order.

The plants went westward with the development of the country. Today the company still operates facilities in [1]Delaware, [2]Illinois, [3]California, and [4]Colorado. (Since California became a state before Colorado, this sequence may be correct. If the sequence is strictly geographical, then Colorado and California should be transposed.)

Paragraph (¶ , no ¶). Each paragraph should be a self-contained unit of related ideas. Break up paragraphs that contain too many ideas; join paragraphs where the ideas belong next to one another.

PARAGRAPH

It was stated that the present pay system included both hourly wage and piece work rates but that piece workers quit as early as hourly wage workers; i.e., the incentive pay system did not work. A possible cause of failure was the on-again off-again nature of the incentive resulting from the different pay systems employed on the various ships. A bonus incentive system also existed for supervisors, but it, too, appeared to cause confusion. ¶ One possible solution to the problem would be change entirely to an incentive pay system with management and labor working together to set objective standards . . . .

NO PARAGRAPH

Tabloid newspapers often use single-sentence paragraphs.
  no ¶ They believe that readers find it easier to understand one sentence at a time.
  no ¶ However, close examination shows that simple sentences often fit together without the need for spacing.

Transition (trans). Faulty transitions obscure the relationship between one sentence or paragraph and the next. Some writers pick up a word from the previous sentence and repeat that word (or a synonym) in the next sentence. Do not use this device all the time, or your writing will become mechanical. Also, do not use conjunctive adverbs like *however* and *nevertheless* at the beginning of paragraphs because these words only connect single thoughts and not entire arguments.

  . . . . Thus, in order to compete, American railroads must *modernize*. *Modernization* challenges the American auto industry as well . . . .

Format

Citation style. Most professions have created their own citation styles for accurate references. If you are unsure of the style in your field, consult a professional journal or a style book like Turabian's *A Manual for Writers,* 4th ed. (Chicago, 1973). Remember, unnecessary citations, whether footnotes, end notes, or internal citations, distract a reader. Be accurate and complete, but not pedantic.

INTERNAL CITATION

For internal citations use parentheses (or brackets [when necessary]) and limit the information included:

1 The new *MLA Handbook* (1977) revises footnote style.

2 Stevens (1968) has proposed a theory that only a few writers have disputed (Jackson, Quint, and Worker, 1978).

FOOTNOTES OR END NOTES

Footnotes usually are placed at the bottom of a page and end notes at the end of a chapter, although citations at the end of a chapter can still be called footnotes.

For citations, use a superscript number at the end of the material to be cited (place punctuation before the number).[1] For longer works, begin each chapter with "1." Long footnotes of opinion or explanation either belong in the text or are digressive and should be eliminated. Use footnotes for documentation. As Fenton Forbes said, "Footnotes are the roots of the scholarly tree."[2]

Headings. Headings and subheads contribute to clarity by signifying each section's degree of importance.

In articles, reports, memos, résumés—any long piece of writing—each topic should have the same kind of heading, descending in importance from all capitals of various sizes to boldface and italics. Too many subcategories will confuse readers, but if headings and subcategories are consistent, you will give readers clear signs to guide them through the text.

HEADINGS AND SUBHEADS

Construction Materials Industries

PORTLAND CEMENT

Market structure . . . .
Current trends . . . .

Spelling and Capitalization

Spelling (sp). Bad spelling is the sign of sloppy thinking or, worse, unprofessional carelessness. Those who admit to being bad spellers (some even take pride in their errors) avoid learning the few rules that will help eliminate the embarrassment of shoddy work.

The easiest way to become a good speller is to write down the words you misspell most often, find the correct spelling, and memorize. Here is an arbitrary list of ten commonly misspelled words. Add ten more that give you trouble. Verify the spelling and meaning of all twenty words in a dictionary. Consult a dictionary so that you can check to see if you are using the right word. Then spend as much time as you need to eliminate twenty of your greatest embarrassments.

---

[1] For examples of documentation (books, articles, magazines, etc.), see the bibliography of this book.
[2] *Seven Ways to Become a Scholar* (Los Angeles: Fulcort Press, 1985), p. 896. (Note: Forbes and his *magnum opus* are fictitious.)

TEN COMMONLY MISSPELLED WORDS

accommodate	occasion
apparent	occurrence
consensus	relevant
embarrass	separate
liaison	supersede

To become a good speller you need not memorize every word or look up every word in a dictionary. Learning some simple rules of syllabification will help avoid constant misspelling. (Knowing Latin is also useful!)

RULES OF SYLLABIFICATION

Rule 1   Separate prefixes from roots.
mis + spell = misspell
dis + ap + pear = disappear

Rule 2   Separate suffixes from roots, eliminatıng the final silent *e* before a vowel. Double the consonant if the root is accented or if the word has only one syllable (the consonant *s* is excepted).
come + ing = coming
oc + cur + rence = occurrence
fat + ter = fatter
bus + es = buses

Rule 3   Split words between syllables. (Never split roots or single-syllable words.)
dis-ap-pear (not dis-app-ear)
glove (not gl-ove)

THE APOSTROPHE

The apostrophe (') is used to signify either the possessive or a contraction.

The Possessive   Singular nouns: place the apostrophe between the last letter and the *s*: "the book's cover." Plural nouns: place the apostrophe after the last letter even if that letter is an *s*: "James' book; the books' covers." (British usage and some American editors require an *s* after the apostrophe: "James's books."

Contractions   The apostrophe stands for letters left out of words: don't = do not; we'll = we will; they're = they are.

In formal writing do not use contractions because the tone becomes informal, and do not confuse the spelling and meaning of *it*:

its = possessive: It has its moments.

it's = contraction for it is: It's difficult to remember all the rules.

Capitalization (cap).   In German, common nouns are capitalized, and until the eighteenth century many common nouns in English were capitalized. In modern English, only proper nouns are capitalized unless the common noun clearly refers to a unique entity (the President) or has always been capitalized by an organization. Exceptions to the rule are determined by an organization's editorial policy or *house style.*

Capitalize for clarity; do not overcapitalize.

Error	Correction
The *D*ivision *H*ead asked all *C*ompany employees to contribute to the United Fund.	The *d*ivision *h*ead asked all *c*ompany employees to contribute to the United Fund.

Punctuation

Punctuation helps make sense out of a jumble. Punctuation marks signify pauses and divide sentences into logical units.

COMMA (,)

Explanation	Example
Use a comma	
1. To set aside a word or phrase	The president, an active man, rides horses.
2. To mark off elements in a series	The flag was red, white, and blue.
[Opinions vary on whether the last element in a series should be preceded by a comma. Comma or not, always be consistent.]	
3. To divide independent clauses separated by a coordinating conjunction	The rain was coming down harder, but the game continued.
4. To set off a nonrestrictive clause introduced by *which* or *who*	The computer program, which was new, created problems for the staff.
	The consultant, who was hired last week, recommended several changes.
Do not use a comma	
1. To separate compound nouns or verbs	He waited as long as he could [no comma] and left without seeing the doctor.
2. To introduce a dependent clause	The copy machine [no comma] that needs repair is next to the watercooler.
3. To create an unnatural pause, especially between noun and verb	The first few words of a speech [no comma] are important for establishing tone.

SEMICOLON (;)

Explanation	Example
Use a semicolon	
1. To separate independent clauses without conjunctions	The project was successful; the company made money for the first time.
2. To separate independent clauses joined by conjunctive adverbs (however, nevertheless, moreover, etc.)	The building was new; however, all the walls were cracking.
3. To separate elements of a series following a colon where there is other internal punctuation (Unlike comma usage, a semicolon is *always* placed before the last element of a series.)	A persuasive memo contains four sections: first, background or history; second, current situation; third, solutions (including the best one); and fourth, recommendation for action.

COLON (:)

Explanation	Example
Use a colon	
1. To introduce a list (a comma is used for a simple list; a semicolon is used when the item includes more than one phrase or clause)	The shipment includes the following items: overhead projector, videotape recorder, monitor, camera, and tapes.
2. To call attention to what follows (the colon functions like the word *namely*)	One punctuation mark calls attention to what follows: the colon.

DASH (—)

Explanation	Example
The dash is not an all-purpose punctuation mark. Use it, almost like an arrow	
1. To set aside important information within a sentence	Three steps—research, organization and revision—are essential to writing.
2. To introduce information (functions like a colon)	When giving a speech, follow these rules—analyze audience, organize material logically, rehearse until smooth.

Do not use the dash to replace commas, semicolons, or even periods.

PARENTHESES ()

Explanation	Example

The dash calls out; the parenthesis encloses.
Use parentheses

1. To list numbers

Communication skills include: (1) reading; (2) writing; (3) listening; and (4) speaking.

2. To make an informal citation

The two New York blackouts (1965, 1977) were a danger signal to our country.

3. To make an aside to the reader

He knew (all too well) that he couldn't finish in time.

BRACKETS []

Explanation	Example

1. To add an editor's note

Don't make no [sic] mistakes.

2. To amend a mistake

Don't make [any] mistakes.

3. To act as parentheses within parentheses

Several energy breakdowns (New York blackouts [1965, 1977], Three Mile Island [1979]) still require further explanation.

ELLIPSES (. . . OR . . . .)

Explanation	Example

Ellipses signify material taken out of quotation.
Use

1. Three dots separated by spaces (. . .) to eliminate part of a sentence

"Several energy breakdowns . . . still require further explanation."

2. Four dots separated by spaces (. . . .) to eliminate one or more complete sentences

"Oh, say can you see . . . . the home of the brave."

When beginning a quotation in the middle of a sentence, it is not necessary to use ellipses.

SLASH OR VIRGULE (/)

Explanation	Example
Use the slash	
1. To signify alternatives	Accommodations are free; rail/air transportation is extra.
2. To join periods of time	The meetings took place in May/June of 1984.

The slash is shorthand. For clarity, use words and not signs.

QUOTATION MARKS (". . . .")

Explanation	Example
Use quotation marks	
1. To surround words quoted exactly (Do not use quotation marks to paraphrase.)	"Economic recovery is imminent," the minister declared.
2. To indicate unusual usage	The new computer is "user-friendly."
3. To indicate all titles except books and plays which are underlined	"Politics and the English Language" is contained in the book, *A Collection of Essays by George Orwell.*

Put periods and commas inside quotation marks; colons, semicolons, and other marks outside.

Proofreading

Careless mistakes give the impression of a careless mind. As any writer knows, proofreading is a very difficult skill to learn. Here are some suggestions.

1   Read a page twice, once from the top down and then from the bottom up.

2   Sound out the important words as you read to yourself.

3   Double-check dates and figures.

4   Beware of the sin of omission as well as commission.

5   Use two people for the final proofreading. Have one person read a copy out loud and the other mark errors. Then reverse the jobs. Good writers never sign their names to a document without *trying* to achieve perfection! Look for trouble before others find it.

To help you edit your own work and the work of others, refer to the following abbreviated list of proofreading symbols.

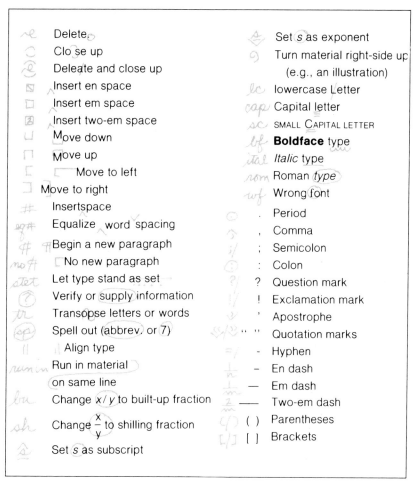

Delete		Set *s* as exponent
Close up		Turn material right-side up
Deleate and close up		(e.g., an illustration)
Insert en space	*lc*	lowercase Letter
Insert em space	*cap*	Capital letter
Insert two-em space	*sc*	SMALL CAPITAL LETTER
Move down	*bf*	**Boldface** type
Move up	*ital*	*Italic* type
Move to left	*rom*	Roman *type*
Move to right	*wf*	Wrong font
Insertspace		. Period
Equalize word spacing		, Comma
Begin a new paragraph		; Semicolon
No new paragraph		: Colon
Let type stand as set		? Question mark
Verify or supply information		! Exclamation mark
Transopse letters or words		' Apostrophe
Spell out (abbrev. or 7)		" " Quotation marks
Align type		- Hyphen
Run in material		– En dash
on same line		— Em dash
Change *x/y* to built-up fraction		—— Two-em dash
Change $\frac{x}{y}$ to shilling fraction		( ) Parentheses
Set *s* as subscript		[ ] Brackets

Figure A-1   Proofreading symbols.

Source: Marie M. Longyear, ed., *The McGraw-Hill Style Manual* (New York: McGraw-Hill, 1983).

APPENDIX 2

Workshops on Writing and Speaking

Advice is meaningful if you can apply it to your own situation. The directions and examples in this book should help you identify problems of writing and speaking and should cause you to think about ways to improve your communication skills. The following exercises will enable you to practice common forms of communication.

Six Sessions on Writing

SESSION I—COMMON SENTENCE FAULTS

Analyze the following sentences for grammar, syntax, ambiguity, and wordiness. Circle errors, name them, and correct them. If necessary, rewrite the sentences, but do not change the meaning.

1   Empirical investigations into the optimal financial structure of a firm and the use of the capital asset pricing model for investment analysis have firmly established their statistical validity for domestic firms.

2 Too many variables are left untreated that have important impacts on profits.

3 Prior experience and current knowledge is completely neglected.

4 The end result of the process is a unit price and warranty period that arises without requiring the competence and gut feelings of the final decision makers.

5 The restrictions upon Plaintiff's mental and bodily privacy were no greater than necessary to effect his rehabilitation through aversive conditioning.

6 Having no contact with subordinates, these preconceived notions of worker incompetency will grow rather than diminish because management will encounter no experience on which to base attitude changes.

7 The proceeds from the sale would be large, which I realized almost immediately.

8 The answer lies in forcing officer analyst interaction with the aim of utilizing the skills and expertise available to the organization to the fullest extent.

9 The IRS, in giving its opinion about the new addition, says that it must be considered a part of the old building.

10 The President of the Division issued orders to reduce staff, increased productivity, developing new products, however he expected problems in complying.

SESSION II—PARAGRAPH REORGANIZATION

The following paragraph is unified by a common theme, but the ideas do not fit together coherently. Reorganize the paragraph, creating new transitions where necessary.

Around 1900 an attempt was made to use steel as the major construction element in three large dams. However, after the failure of the Hauser Lake Dam, the idea was generally abandoned. Today steel dams are used only as temporary cofferdams needed for construction of permanent dams. Basically a framework covered with riveted steel plate is used for the steel dam. A masonry abutment is used to anchor the steel work into the reservoir. A typical design is shown in Figure 19. The Hauser Lake Dam in Montana failed on April 14, 1908. Steel dams decreased in popularity after this. There were only three major steel dams made. These were the aforementioned Hauser Lake Dam, the Red Ridge Dam in Michigan, and the Ash Fork dam in Arizona. The basic design of these dams can be seen in Figure 20. The small number of these dams that were built made stability design a matter of calculation rather than experience. The Hauser Lake Dam failed due to over-turning.[1]

SESSION III—DEFINITION OF A COMMON TERM

Technical terms can be confusing if writer and reader (speaker and listener) do not know the specific meaning of a particular term. We often take for granted that everyone knows what we are talking about. In order to clarify your thinking and to be able to explain difficult terms precisely, select a technical term you use everyday and write an extended definition. Begin with a formal definition: name the term, its class, and what makes it different from other terms in its class. (Cryogenic finishing is a process of supercooling used to deflash molded rubber or plastic products.) After the formal explanation write an extended definition by giving examples, showing uses, or creating contrasts.

Write the definition for one of two audiences: those who have a thorough knowledge of the general subject or those who know nothing about it. As an additional exercise, write a second definition for the audience you did not originally select.

SAMPLE DEFINITION
CRYOGENIC FINISHING

Cryogenic Finishing is a process used to deflash molded rubber and plastic products. Cryogenic refers to the use of gases supercooled to a liquid state, and finishing refers to the act of deflashing.

Many of the molds used to make rubber and plastic products have an upper and a lower half. During the molding process heated material is forced into these molds to fill cavities cut in the mold to the shape of the product. Some of the heated material will seep between the mold halves, outside of the product cavities. This excess material will remain on the product as flash when the product is removed from the mold. This flash must be removed to get a finished product.

After the product is removed from the mold it can be cryo-genically deflashed by one of two methods: tumbling or shot blasting. For tumbling, the product is put into a tumbling chamber and liquid nitrogen at a temperature of $-320°F$ is sprayed onto the parts. This supercold liquid immediately embrittles the flash. As the

[1]Deborah C. Andrews and Margaret D. Blickle, *Technical Writing: Principles and Forms*, 2d ed. (New York: Macmillan, 1982), p. 91.

parts tumble, the embrittled flash is broken off. The process of shot blasting is basically the same, except that in lieu of tumbling, plastic shot is hurled on the parts breaking off the flash.

SESSION IV—TONE

The tone of a letter often conveys emotions or attitudes that influence meaning. Select a subject like a request for a raise or a complaint. Determine your audience and write a letter in the appropriate tone (informal, formal, deferential, factual). Write the same letter several times, using a variety of tones.

SESSION V—MEMO

Write a memo using a visual format:

```
TO:
FROM:
SUBJECT:
DATE:
                I.    Background
               II.    Current situation
              III.    Solution
               IV.    Recommendation
```

Vary this suggested format according to topic and audience, but use headlines so that the reader can immediately abstract the meaning of your memo.

SESSION VI—EDITING

Edit the following writing sample. Use common editing symbols (see Appendix I).

This article suggests that the economic problems of America are due just as much to an inability to accomodate to social changes as they are due to business slowdown. Further, the article suggests that one of the solutions to these problems lie in the future relationship between management and labor. The traditional association between these two groups has been adversarial, but the current recession may be an effective catalyst forcing these two bodies to reexamine their relationship and begin developing new cooperative alliances which would serve long term mutual interests of both instead of short term demands of one or the other. Two of the possible products of an effective union-management alliance would be an enrichment of employee worklife experiences and an expansion of the ways that management and union relate to each other. Resolving confilcts would cease to be the only reason for these groups to interact.

Six Sessions on Speaking

SESSION I—DICTION

Speaking clearly prevents slurring of words and allows an audience to concentrate on what you say rather than on how you speak. Using a tape recorder, practice the following two diction exercises until the words are clear and the sentences convey the meaning intended by the author.

1. The President reported that new business development will be costly.

2. In our time, political speech and writing are largely the defence of the indefensible. Things like the continuance of British rule in India, the Russian purges and deportations, the dropping of the atom bombs on Japan, can indeed be defended, but only by arguments which are too brutal for most people to face, and which do not square with the professed aims of political parties. Thus political language has to consist largely of euphemism, question-begging, and sheer cloudy vagueness. Defenceless villages are bombarded from the air, the inhabitants driven out into the countryside, the cattle machine-gunned, the huts set on fire with incendiary bullets: this is called pacification. Millions of peasants are robbed of their farms and sent trudging along the roads with no more than they can carry: this is called transfer of population or rectification of frontiers. People are imprisoned for years without trial, or shot in the back of the neck or sent to die of scurvy in Arctic lumber camps; this is called elimination of unreliable elements. Such phraseology is needed if one wants to name things without calling up mental pictures of them. Consider for instance some comfortable English professor defending Russian totalitarianism. He cannot say outright, "I believe in killing off your opponents when you can get good results by doing so." Probably, therefore, he will say something like this:

"While freely conceding that the Soviet régime exhibits certain features which the humanitarian may be inclined to deplore, we must, I think, agree that a certain curtailment of the right to political opposition is an unavoidable concomitant of transitional periods, and that the rigors which the Russian people have been called upon to undergo have been amply justified in the sphere of concrete achievement."

George Orwell
"Politics and the English
Language" (1946)

SESSION II—IMPROMPTU SPEAKING

We are often called on to give a brief introduction, synopsis, or explanation. Even though you may have little or no time to prepare, you can organize your thoughts quickly so that they make sense. For brief impromptu speeches, think first of your conclusion and then fill in the introduction, supporting ideas, and summary. Prepare the three types of speeches suggested below, and present them to an audio or video recorder or to an interested audience.

1   The Virtues of My Hometown

2   Summary of Current Business Activities

3   Introduction of the Main Speaker at an Annual Meeting

SESSION III—PREPARATION

When you have more than a minute to prepare a speech, you need to develop a style for creating a manuscript that you find easy to use. Practice several styles. Select one that is most comfortable, but be prepared to use others. The following exercises will help you determine the type of manuscript or notes best-suited to you.

1   Prepare a full topic outline on 8½- by 11-inch sheets of paper. (See Chapter 2.) Add important phrases or sentences to the outline and underline the words or ideas you wish to emphasize. Mark the outline for pauses or appropriate gestures.

2   Prepare the outline of a speech using 3- by 5-inch or 4- by 6-inch cards. Organize all cards in the proper sequence of major category, subcategory, specific examples, etc. Number all cards and mark them as you would an outline on a sheet of paper.

3   Prepare a brief speech written out word for word. Practice reading it aloud. Then make an outline on 8½- by 11-inch sheets of paper or on cards, and

record the speech. Decide which style suits you, remembering that if you are "tied" to manuscript or notes you will not have enough time to establish un-interrupted communication with the audience.

SESSION IV—VISUAL AIDS

When discussing financial data or technical topics, visual support will show an audience what you are telling them. Even if you can rely on professional graphic artists, you should supply a rough idea of what you want to show. Make up the following visual aids and use them in a brief speech. (See Chapter 14.)

1 Bar graph, line graph, pie chart
2 Table of financial data
3 Illustration of an object
4 Outline of a process

SESSION V—PERSUASIVE SPEECH

One of the reasons for communicating is to motivate people to do something. Review principles of logic (see Chapter 3), and prepare a speech on one or more of the following topics.

1 Why You Should Give to the United Fund

2 Why Our Company Should Develop a New Product

3 Why You Should Buy Our New Product

SESSION VI—ANSWERING QUESTIONS

The end of a formal presentation is usually a question-and-answer period. Anticipating questions and planning answers can give you confidence and show the audience that you know what you are talking about from introduction to conclusion. Select a topic, prepare and rehearse a speech, and then make a list of questions you think you will be asked and of answers you would like to give. Organize questions and answers in the following categories.

1 General definition of terms

2 Relationship to other phenomena (similarities, differences)

3 Problems

4 Costs

5 Uses and benefits

Bibliography

Bibliographies provide a list of works cited and works consulted. Most bibliographies *select* the titles that will help the reader continue research. Bibliographies can list all entries alphabetically, or they can be divided by topic, by chapter or major section, or by types: books (reference books, texts, anthologies, monographs) and periodicals.

The following bibliography includes works cited in the text, works consulted for background information, and works helpful for further reference.

Alvarez, Joseph A. *The Elements of Technical Writing.* New York: Harcourt Brace Jovanovich, 1980.

Anderson, Virgil A. *Training the Speaking Voice.* 3d ed. New York: Oxford University Press, 1977.

Andrews, Clarence A. *Technical and Business Writing.* Boston: Houghton Mifflin, 1975.

Andrews, Deborah C. and Margaret D. Blickle. *Technical Writing: Principles and Forms.* 2d ed. New York: Macmillan, 1982.

Bacon, Francis. *Essays.* New York: Dutton, 1907.

Berry, Thomas Elliott. *The Craft of Writing.* New York: McGraw-Hill, 1974.

Briden, Earl F. "The Jargonist as Comedian." *ABCA Bulletin,* 45, March 1982, pp. 39–41.

Brusaw, Charles T., Gerald J. Alred, and Walter E. Oliu. *The Business Writer's Handbook.* 2d ed. New York: St. Martin's Press, 1982.

Computer-Readable Databases: A Directory and Data Sourcebook. Urbana, IL: American Society for Information Science, 1982.

Crews, Frederick. *The Random House Handbook.* 3d ed. New York: Random House, 1980.

Directory of Online Information Resources. Kensington, MD: CSG Press, 1983.

Elbow, Peter. *Writing with Power.* New York: Oxford University Press, 1981.

Fadiman, Clifton and James Howard. *Empty Pages: A Search for Writing Competence in School and Society.* Belmont, CA: Fearon Pitman, 1979.

Flesch, Rudolf. *The Art of Plain Talk*. New York: Macmillan, 1962.

Follett, Wilson. *Modern American Usage*. Ed. Jacques Barzun. New York: Hill and Wang (Warner Books), 1966.

Glatthorn, Alan A. and Herbert R. Adams. *Listening Your Way to Management Success*. Glenview, IL: Scott, Foresman, 1983.

Golen, Steven P., Ross Figgins, and Larry R. Smeltzer. *Readings and Cases in Business Communication*. New York: Wiley, 1984.

Harty, Kevin. *Strategies for Business and Technical Writing*. New York: Harcourt Brace Jovanovich, 1980.

Hawkins, Brian L. and Paul Preston. *Managerial Communication*. Santa Monica, CA: Goodyear, 1981.

Himstreet, William C. and Wayne M. Baty. *Business Communications: Principles and Methods*. 7th ed. Boston: Kent, 1984.

Hodges, John C. and Mary E. Whitten. *Harbrace College Handbook*. 8th ed. New York: Harcourt Brace Jovanovich, 1977.

Holcombe, Marya A. and Judith K. Stein. *Writing for Decision Makers*. Belmont, CA: Lifetime Learning Publications, 1981.

————. *Presentations for Decision Makers*. Belmont, CA: Lifetime Learning Publications, 1983.

Holtz, Herman. *Persuasive Writing*. New York: McGraw-Hill, 1983.

Irmscher, William F. *The Holt Guide to English*. New York: Holt, Rinehart, & Winston, 1972.

Jones, Stanley E., Dean C. Barnlund, and Franklyn S. Haiman. *The Dynamics of Discussion: Communication in Small Groups*. 2d ed. New York: Harper & Row, 1980.

Lanham, Richard. *Revising Business Prose*. New York: Scribner's, 1981.

Lesikar, Raymond V. *Business Communication: Theory and Application*. 4th ed. Homewood, IL: Richard D. Irwin, 1980.

Lindauer, Jacqueline. *Communicating in Business*. Philadelphia: Saunders, 1979.

Management Contents. Northbrook, IL: Management Contents, 1974—.

Management Contents Data Base Thesaurus. Northbrook, IL: Management Contents, Inc., 1981.

Mathes, J. C. and Dwight W. Stevenson. *Technical Reports*. Indianapolis: Bobbs-Merrill, 1976.

Minnick, Wayne C. *Public Speaking*. Boston: Houghton Mifflin, 1979.

Monroe, Alan and Douglas Ehninger. *Principles of Speech Communication*. 8th ed. Glenview, IL: Scott, Foresman, 1980.

Munter, Mary. *Guide to Managerial Communication*. Englewood Cliffs, NJ: Prentice-Hall, 1982.

Murphy, Herta A. and Herbert W. Hildebrandt. *Effective Business Communications*. 4th ed. New York: McGraw-Hill, 1984.

Newman, Edwin. *Strictly Speaking*. New York: Warner Books, 1975.

Nicholson, Margaret. *A Dictionary of American-English Usage based on Fowler's Modern English Usage*. Oxford: Oxford University Press, 1957.

Nolan, Martin. "Write the Way You Wish You Talked." *Washington Journalism Review*, October 1981, p. 60.

Oliu, Walter E., Charles Brusaw, and Gerald J. Alred. *Writing that Works*. New York: St. Martin's Press, 1980.

Oliver, Robert T., Dallas C. Dickey, and Harold P. Zelko. *Communicative Speech*. Rev. ed New York: Dryden Press, 1955.

Orwell, George. *A Collection of Essays*. New York: Harcourt Brace Jovanovich (Harvest), 1953.

Pauley, Steven E. *Technical Report Writing Today*. Boston: Houghton Mifflin, 1979.

Sigband, Norman. *Communication for Management and Business*. 3d ed. Glenview, IL: Scott, Foresman, 1982.

Smeltzer, Larry R. and John L. Waltman. *Managerial Communication: A Strategic Approach*. New York: Wiley, 1984.

Sparrow, W. Keats and Donald H. Cunningham. *The Practical Craft: Readings for Business and Technical Writers*. Boston: Houghton Mifflin, 1978.

Stone, Wilfred and J. G. Bell. *Prose Style: A Handbook for Writers*. 4th ed. New York: McGraw-Hill, 1983.

Strunk, William, Jr. and E. B. White. *The Elements of Style*. 3d ed. New York: Macmillan, 1979.

Thomson, A. J. and A. V. Martinet. *A Practical English Grammar*. 3d ed. Oxford: University Press, 1980.

Timm, Paul R. *Managerial Communication*. Englwood Cliffs, NJ: Prentice-Hall, 1980.

Toulmin, Stephen E. *The Uses of Argument*. Cambridge: Cambridge University Press, 1958.

Tufte, Edward R. *The Visual Display of Quantitative Information*. Cheshire, CT: Graphics Press, 1983.

Turabian, Kate L. *A Manual for Writers*. 4th ed. Chicago: University of Chicago Press, 1973.

Wachter, Michael L. and Susan M. Wachter, eds. *Toward a New U.S. Industrial Policy*? Philadelphia: University of Pennsylvania Press, 1983.

Walsh, J. Martyn and Anna Kathleen Walsh. *Plain English Handbook*. 7th ed. Cincinnati: McCormick-Mathers, 1977.

Webber, Ross. *Management*. Rev. ed. Homewood, IL: Richard D. Irwin, 1979.

Zinsser, William. *On Writing Well*. 2d ed. New York: Harper & Row, 1980.

Acknowledgments

Deborah C. Andrews and Margaret D. Blickle, excerpt from *Teaching Writing: Principles and Forms*, 2d ed., Macmillan Publishing Company, 1982. © 1982 by the Macmillan Publishing Company. Reprinted by permission.

Herb Caen, excerpt from his column in the *San Francisco Chronical.* © 1964 by the *San Francisco Chronicle.* Reprinted by permission.

Thomas Chacko and James C. McElroy, abstract of "The Cognitive Component in Locke's Theory of Goal Setting: Suggestive Evidence for a Causal Attribution Interpretation," *Academy of Management Journal*, 1983, vol. 26, no. 1. Reprinted by permission of the authors and the *Academy of Management Journal.*

Clayton Hill, "Carl Lohman, Lineman." Reprinted by permission of Mrs. Louella Hill.

George Orwell, excerpts from "Politics and the English Language," *A Collection of Essays*, Harcourt Brace Jovanovich (Harvest). © 1953 by Sonia Brownell Orwell. Reprinted by permission.

Stephen E. Toulmin, excerpt from *The Uses of Argument*, Oxford University Press, 1964. © 1964 by Oxford University Press. Reprinted by permission.

Ross A. Webber, excerpt from *Management*, rev. ed., Richard D. Irwin, Inc., 1979. © 1979 by Richard D. Irwin, Inc. Reprinted by permission.

Index

Abstract(s), 9, 15, 89–90, 96
Action step, 137
Adjectives, 52
Administrative Management Society, 64
Adverbs, 52
Agendas, 176–179
Agreement:
  antecedent/pronoun, 47, 189
  subject/verb, 45, 189
Ambiguity, 47, 193
Apostrophe, 200
Appearance, 182
  (*See also* Dress)
Aristotelian logic, 35
Audience:
  analyzing needs of, 131
  attitudes toward: deference, 25
    honesty, 25
  awareness of, 143
  of a case analysis, 107
  determining, 24, 100, 208
  in group presentations, 165, 167
  involving, 42
  level of knowledge of, 24
  of a memo, 75, 85
  primary, 4, 13, 45, 75, 85, 107
  profile of, 25
  relationship of speaker to, 150, 159–160

Audience (*Cont.*):
  of a report, 86–87
  secondary, 4, 13, 45, 75, 85
Awkward syntax, 194

Bacon, Francis, 12–13, 35
Barriers to communication, 9–12, 83
  ethical standards as, 11
  organizational: between peers, 11
    between subordinates and superiors, 11
    between superiors and subordinates, 10–11
  personal: stage fright, 10, 143–145
    writer's block, 9–10, 17, 21
  visual aids as, 159
Beginning of a speech, 132–133
Bibliography, 213–215
  in reports, 95
Blackboard, use of, 158
Block style in letters, 61, 62, 64
Body:
  of a letter, 60, 61
  of a report, 91–95
  of a speech, 133–134
Body, use of, 149
Body movement, 141
Brackets, 203

Breathing, 148, 151, 153, 183
Budgets in funding proposals, 104

Cadence, 151
Candidate for job interview, 182
Capitalization, 199–201
Case as grammatical term, 190
Case analysis, 106–116
  audience of, 107
  format of, 108
  outline of, 106–107
  sample, 108–114
  simulated, 114–116
  summary of, 108
Case statement, 102
Chart, sample, 158
Checklist:
  for controlling stage fright, 145
  for giving group presentations, 167–168
  for rehearsing, 142
  for rereading, 45
Ciceronian oratory, 135
Citation style, 198–199
Clauses:
  nonrestrictive, 53
  relative, 53
  restrictive, 53
Clichés, 48
College interview, 181, 185, 187–188
Colon, 202
Comma, 201
Comma fault, 191
Composition, methods of:
  dictation, 28, 30–31
  longhand, 28–29
  word processing, 29–30
Compound nouns, 52
Compound verbs, 52
Computer as research tool, 18–21, 32
  databases, 18–19
  hit ratio in literature search, 19
  key words, 19
  printouts, 19
Conclusion:
  in job interviews, 186
  of a speech, 134–135
Consultant's report, 107, 112
Correcting, 45
Courtesy, 179
Curriculum Vitae, 117

Dangling modifier, 191
Dash, 202
Data sheet, 117
Deductive logic, 34, 36–37, 41, 43,
  133
Defining terms, 32
Definition:
  extended, 208
  formal, 208
Delivery of a speech, 141
  techniques of, 143–153
Development proposal, 108
  (*See also* Funding proposals)
Dewey, John, 136
Diction:
  enunciation, 141, 149, 153, 178, 210
  word choice, 8, 48–49, 194
    abstract, 49
    polysyllabic Latinate, 49
    pretentious, 49
Dossier, 117
Drawings, 155
Dress, 146, 151, 182, 185

Easel, 157, 158
Editing, 209
Effective speaking, principles of, 169
Ellipses, 203
End notes, 198
  (*See also* Footnotes)
Enunciation, 141, 149, 153, 178, 210
Ethics, 10–11
Euphemism, 53, 210
Evaluation interview, 181, 186
Eye contact, 10, 144–145, 152, 179
Executive summary, 112–114
Exit interview, 181, 186

Fair employment practice laws, 121
Fielden, John, 13
Filmstrips, 158
Flip charts, 159
Follow-up to job interview, 184
Food to avoid before speaking, 146
Footnotes, 95, 198–199
  and end notes, distinction between, 198
Format:
  citation style, 198
  footnotes or end notes, 198–199
  headings, 199

Function of communication:
  implementing, 12
  organizing, 12
  succeeding, 12–13
Fund appeals, 42
Funding proposals, 100–104
  budgets in, 104
  to foundations, corporations, or individuals,
      100–101
  sample summary, 102–104
  (*See also* Proposals)

Gestures, 140, 147, 149, 152
Glossary of style and usage, 189–205
Grammar, 46, 189–193
  in résumés, 124
Graphic material:
  in visual aids, 155–159, 161
  in written documents, 92–94
Group communication, 5, 6
Group presentations, 165–170
  audience in, 165, 167
  checklist for giving, 167–168
  preparation for, 167
  purpose in, 165, 167
  rehearsing for, 166–168
  topic for, 167, 169

Hands, 149
Heading(s):
  of a memo, 76, 77
  in a report, 91
  in résumés, 122
  in written documents, 77, 199
Honesty:
  in answering questions, 173
  as approach to audience, 25
House style, 76

Illustrations, 155
Impersonal construction, 191
Impromptu speaking, 152, 211
Inductive logic, 35–37, 41, 43, 133
Inflection, 149
Information interviews, 181, 186
Informative communication:
  general description in conveying
      information, 14–16, 24
  in speaking, 131, 133–135
Interpersonal communication, 4–6
Interviewer, responsibilities of, 187

Interviews:
  college, 181, 185, 187–188
  evaluation, 181, 186
  exit, 181, 186
  information, 181, 186
  job (*see* Job interview)
  newspaper, 186

Jargon, 48, 194–195
Job interview, 181–185, 187
  inquiry letter for, 70
  and job performance, 186
  questions asked in, 183, 184

Leadership:
  in meetings, 177
  styles of, 165, 166
Length of résumé, 124–125
Letterhead, 60
Letters:
  audience of, 59
  of complaint, 73
  components of: address of respondent, 60
      address of writers, 60
      body, 60, 61
      complimentary close, 60–62
      letterhead, 60
      reference, 60, 62–63
      salutation, 60–61, 63
      signature, 62
  formal, 59
  format of, 59–64
  informal, 59
  informative, 66
  inquiry, 64–65, 72
  job inquiry, 70–73
  layout of: block style, 63
      modified block style, 63–64
  persuasive, 67
  problem-solving, 67
  purpose for writing, 59
  sales, 68–70, 73
  tone of, 59, 61, 65, 72, 73, 209
Levels of communication:
  group, 5, 6
  interpersonal, 4–6
Listening, 5–6, 181, 187
Literature search:
  computerized, 32
  databases for, 18–20
  printed, 18, 20

Logic, 7, 24–38, 50, 106, 144, 197
  in answering questions, 172
  Aristotelian, 35
  deductive, 34, 36–37, 41, 43, 133
  inductive, 35–37, 41, 43, 133
  in meetings, 176
  syllogism, 34–35, 197
  testing, 36, 197
  variations of: cause and effect, 37
    comparison and contrast, 37
    Toulmin model, 37, 43

Manuscript preparation, 139–140
Meetings, 176–180
  formal, 176
  participating in, 178–179
  preparation for, 176
  running, 177
Memos, 74–85
  audience of, 75, 85
  business, 45
  ending, 77
  to the file or record, 74, 75, 85
  format of, 76, 209
  headings of, 76, 77
  of information, 15, 74, 78–80, 85
  of inquiry, 74
  length of, 78
  of persuasion, 16, 74, 81–83, 85
  topic of, 78
Metaphor(s), 195–196
  overuse of, 50
Modifiers:
  dangling, 191
  faulty, 47
  imprecise, 48
  misplaced, 191
Monroe, Alan, 136
  motivated sequence developed by, 136, 138
Mood, 192
Movies as visual aid, 159
Ms. salutation, 60

Names, use of, in job interviews, 183
Newspaper interview, 186
"Noise" preventing clear communication, 3–4
Noun phrases, 51
Noun strings, 51

Objective of résumé, 118–119
  aggressive, 119
  limiting, 119
  meaningless, 119
  (*See also* Résumés)
Organization, 5, 7–8, 38–41, 45–46, 131–139, 197–198
  paragraph, 39–41
  plan of: categorical, 38
    causal, 38
    sequential, 38
    spatial, 38
  of a speech, 131–138
Outline:
  of a case analysis, 106–107
  format of: arabic numerals, 23–24
    capitalizing, 23
    roman numerals, 22–23
    spacing, 23
  sentence, 21
  simple, 21
  of a speech, 139–140
  topic, 22, 32, 211
Overhead projector, 150, 158, 161

Panel discussion, 168, 170
Paragraphs, 39–41, 197–198, 207
Parallel structure, 192
Parallelism, faulty, 47
Parentheses, 203
Parliamentary procedure, 176–178
Partition statement, 133, 135, 138
Performance evaluation, 186
Persuasion, 12, 14, 16–17, 24, 33, 41–42, 131, 136–137
  in group presentations, 168
  in speaking, 133–135, 138, 212
  strategy for, 136–137
Photographs as visual aids, 155
Planning:
  for group presentations, 165, 167
    answers to questions, 166, 169–170
  for interviews, 181
Pleonasm, 54
Posture, 148, 178, 183
Preparation:
  in group presentations, 166–168
  for job interview, 182
  for speaking, 139–142, 144–147, 211
  of visual aids, 156
  (*See also* Rehearsing)

Prepositional phrases, 49, 52
Primary audience, 4, 13, 45, 75, 85, 107
Primary sources of supporting material,
    20
Process of communication, 3–4
Process of revision, 44–56
    (*See also* Revision)
Production of résumés:
    printed, 125
    typed, 125
Pronoun reference, 193
Pronouns, 47
Proofreading, 204
    of résumés, 125
Proofreading symbols, 205
Proposals, 97–105
    components of, 97–98
    for funding, 100–104
    internal, 97
    as persuasive document, 97
    "program profile" 101, 102
    project, 99–100
    sales, 98–99
    summary of, 100
    table of contents, 99
    technical, 99–104
Punctuation, 201–204
    errors of, 47
    in letters: mixed, 62
        open, 62
    in résumés, 124
Purpose:
    in general communication, 14
    in group presentations, 165, 167

Qualifications:
    determining for job interview, 182
    sample for résumé, 119
Questions:
    answering, 212
    asking, 174
    digressions and, 173, 174
    generalizing, 173, 175
    in group presentations, 166, 169–170
    guidelines for answering, 172–174
    hostile, 173–175
    interruptions and, 171
    in job inteviews, 183, 184
    practice in asking and answering, 175
    reinterpreting, 173

Questions (*Cont.*):
    as summary, 174, 175
    understanding, 172
Quotation marks, 204

Received Standard English, 6
Redundancy, 196
Reference, pronoun, 193
References in résumés, 121
Rehearsing:
    checklist for, 142
    for group presentations, 166–168
    for a speech, 139–142
        (*See also* Preparation, for speaking)
    videotaping in, 166
    with visual aids, 157
Relative clauses, 53
Repetition, 196
Reports, 50, 86–96
    abstracts, 89–90, 96
    annual, 87, 189
    appendixes in, 95
    audience of, 86–87
    bibliography in, 95
    body of, 91–95
    documents of transmittal accompanying,
        88–95
    formal, 87
    format of, 87
    headings in, 91
    illustrations and tables in, 89, 92, 94
    informal, 87
    informative, 91
    persuasive, 91
    prefatory parts of, 88–91
    quarterly, 91
    references in, 95
    status, 91
    table of contents of, 89–96
    technical, 91
    title page of, 89
    tone of, 87
    typeface of, 91–92
Request for Proposal (RFP), 99
Rereading, 44–45
    checklist for, 45
Research, 18–21
    general plan of, 139
    for job interviews, 182
Restrictive clauses, 53
Restructuring, 45–46

Résumés, 70–71, 117–128, 189
  chronological, 117, 125, 128
  content of, 118
  Curriculum Vitae, 117
  data sheet, 117
  dossier, 117
  format of, 122–123
  functional, 118, 127, 128
  grammar and punctuation in, 123–125
  length of, 124–125
  margins in, 122
  objective of, 118–119
  production of, 125
  proofreading of, 125
  references in, 121
  spacing in, 122–123
  as summary, 117
Revision, 8, 31–32, 44–56
  process of, 44–56
  sample, 54–56
  of a speech, 141–142
Rewriting, 46
Rhetorical question, 132
Role of case analyst, 107
Room setup, 159–160

Sales documents:
  letters, 68–70, 73, 98
  proposals, 42, 98–99
Salutation in letters, 60–61, 63
Screen placement, 160
Secondary audience, 4, 13, 45, 75, 85
Secondary sources of supporting material, 21
Semicolon, 202
Sentence faults, common, 206–207
Sentence structure, 48–49
Sexism, 61, 76
Slash (virgule), 204
Slide tapes, 158
Slides, 35-mm, 158
Speakers:
  memorable, 146–147
  relationship of, to audience, 150, 159–160
Speech(es):
  checklist for giving, 151–152
  defined, 131
  effective principles of speaking, 169
  impromptu, 152, 211
  organization of, 131–138
  preparation for, 139–142, 144–147, 211

Speech(es) (*Cont.*):
  (*See also specific aspects, for example:*
    Audience; Delivery of a Speech; Group
    presentations; Questions)
Spelling and capitalization, 199–201
Split infinitive, 192
Stage fright, 10, 143–145
  antidotes for, 144
  causes and effects of, 143
  checklist for controlling, 145
Summaries:
  and abstracts, distinction between, 89
  case analysis, 108
  executive, 112–114
  funding proposal, 102–104
  general, 15
  internal, 180
  proposal, 100
  speech, 151
  (*See also* Résumés)
Syllabification, rules of, 200
Syllogism, 34–35, 197
Syntax, 48

Tables, 89, 92, 94, 115
Tense, mixture of, 47
Thesis statement, 9, 132
Tone:
  angry, 26–28
  appropriate, 26, 32–33
  in letters, 59, 61, 65, 72, 73, 209
  respectful, 28
  vocal, 149–150, 153, 183
Topic:
  defining, 17
  in group presentations, 167, 169
  limiting, 17–18
  of a speech, 131
Topic outline, 22, 32, 211
Topic sentence, 39, 46
Topic statement, 132
Toulmin, Stephen, 37, 43
Transitions:
  in group presentations, 169
  in writing, 39, 41, 46, 141, 166, 169, 198
Transparencies, overhead, 160
Trouble in job interviews, 184

Usage, 193–197

Vagueness, 47–48
Verb phrases, 50
Verbs:
  active, 50–51
  passive, 49, 51
  static, 50
Videotapes, 158
  for rehearsals, 166
Visual aids, 140, 150, 154–161, 212
  graphics, 155–159, 161
  in group presentations, 166
  samples, 157
  screen placement, 160
  time of visibility, 156
  types of equipment, 158–159
  words in, 155

Visualization, 16, 67–68, 82, 99–100, 104, 108,
  134, 137
Vocal variety, 150, 152
Voice:
  projection of, 141, 148, 150, 152, 153, 178,
    183
  use of, 149–150

Word choice, 8, 48–49, 194
  abstract, 49
  polysyllabic Latinate, 49
  pretentious, 49
Word processing, 29–30
Wordiness, 50
Writer's block, 9–10, 17, 21
Wrong word, 196–197